Some people point from shores of sa
sibility. But once in a while God raise
to do more than just talk about d.
wade into the middle of the miraculous, their faith leaving a w...
that will impact generations, starting here and now. My friend William McDowell is a waymaker and walking evidence that the move of God isn't coming; it's happening!

—STEVEN FURTICK
NEW YORK TIMES BEST-SELLING AUTHOR
PASTOR, ELEVATION CHURCH

Many people do a God thing without God; that is the definition of *religion*. My friend William is the exact opposite. He refuses to continue going through the Christian motions without seeing and hearing from God. His relentless pursuit has been seen and rewarded, as God continues to pour out His presence, miracles, and a sound that takes us all into God's presence. I thank God for who William is to the kingdom of God at large and to the people who are privileged to call him friend.

—JONATHAN STOCKSTILL
LEAD PASTOR, BETHANY CHURCH

I've known Pastor William McDowell for twenty-five years. We grew up in the same city, both raised by single mothers who wouldn't stop pushing us toward Jesus. I knew God would take William's heart and gift around the world. It was inevitable. But what I did not anticipate was the level of glory that would be unleashed once Pastor William said yes to leading Deeper Fellowship Church.

God wants glory in the local church. It is what Jesus came to establish. (See Matthew 16.) The power, the beauty, the consistency of spiritual growth and development coupled with tangible miracles, signs, and wonders are the heart of the New Testament church. What God is doing in Orlando, Florida, is unprecedented but shouldn't be unexpected. It's what God intended for the local church. May God give us the blueprint for glory to return to His house through the glorious testimonies of God's grace and power in this book.

—JOHN GRAY
PASTOR, RELENTLESS CHURCH

Not only is William a friend, but he has been a mentor to me over the past few years, and I cannot wait for the words of God written in this book to flow through your heart, mind, body, and spirit. The Holy Spirit is alive and well, not only in this book but in William's life, church, and songs. I pray that before you read this powerful book, you say a prayer for Jesus to open up your heart and soul to the spiritual journey you are about to go on! This journey will be overflowing with joy, tears, and the presence of Jesus from beginning to end. The anointing and presence of God are real!

William, thank you for being an amazing influence not only in my life but also in the lives of others. Jesus put us on this earth to serve, and you are doing that, my friend. Jesus reigns!

—RUSSELL WILSON
QUARTERBACK, SEATTLE SEAHAWKS

When he was a young man sitting in the back of the auditorium in my meetings, William McDowell may have been unknown to me, but he certainly was not unknown to God. It has been a tremendous privilege for me to observe his growth and development in so many different areas—as a husband, a father, a music minister, a pastor, a songwriter, a worshipper, and now as an author.

It is gratifying but not at all surprising to me to see how God is using him, not only as an unusually gifted worship leader but also as a caring and compassionate pastor whose services are characterized by a remarkable demonstration of the supernatural power of God. *It's Happening* will take your faith to the next level as Pastor McDowell shares the extraordinary miracles, signs, and wonders God has performed among his dynamic church family.

—DR. ROD PARSLEY
PASTOR AND FOUNDER, WORLD HARVEST CHURCH

IT'S HAPPENING

WILLIAM McDOWELL

CHARISMA
HOUSE

It's HAPPENING by William McDowell
Published by Charisma House
Charisma Media/Charisma House Book Group
600 Rinehart Road
Lake Mary, Florida 32746
www.charismahouse.com

Cover design by Justin Evans

Visit the author's website at www.williammcdowellmusic.com.

Library of Congress Cataloging-in-Publication Data:
An application to register this book for cataloging has been submitted to the Library of Congress.
International Standard Book Number: 978-1-62999-500-7
E-book ISBN: 978-1-62999-501-4

18 19 20 21 22 — 987654321
Printed in the United States of America

This book is dedicated to my children, Joshua, Olivia, Caleb, Joy, and the one yet to be revealed. I suspect that throughout history, in every generation, a prevailing thought emerges that God doesn't move the way He used to, but you know otherwise. As you get older, you will flip through the pages of this book and be able to say you were there when this happened. But this outpouring is not limited to a particular place or time. Heaven will always respond to those who are hungry. You can experience what we have seen and more if you will cling to these words written and consistently pursue a relationship with God. No one will be able to convince you that God doesn't move this way, because you were there! May you experience more of God in your future than I ever did.

I am also aware that many in the next generation and others in the years to come will read this book. This book is also dedicated to you. Don't allow anyone to convince you that a move of God is something of the past. You can experience it too. Whatever you do, don't stop until you too can say, "It's happening!"

CONTENTS

ACKNOWLEDGMENTS

To my wife, LaTae, your unwavering commitment, support, and partnership are what allow this ministry to happen. What you do that is unseen allows all that is seen. I love you with all my heart.

Jevon Bolden, thank you for your tireless work to help make this book come to life. It was clearly destined to happen this way.

Adrienne Gaines, thank you for your amazing work and incredible patience. You are a true gift to us all.

To my mom, Pauline McDowell, you have intentionally lived your life in a way that allowed me not only to pursue every dream in my heart but more importantly to pursue God. As a result, it's happening! I'm proud to be a part of your legacy.

To Caleb Grant, Jason McMullen, and Jerry Bell, you guys inspire, encourage, challenge, and uphold me every day. It is the greatest joy and privilege to walk with you and serve Deeper Fellowship Church with you. This is our story. I just had the privilege of writing about it. I love you brothers dearly!

To Deeper Fellowship Church, I've never seen a group of people anywhere in the world pursue God the way you do. It's not just a privilege to serve as your pastor; it's an even greater privilege just to be a part of this community. What is happening among us is special. May we never take it for granted. We've only scratched the surface. There's more!

To my pastor, Bishop Joseph Garlington; Pastor Sam Oye; and every pastor, prophetic voice, and lead worshipper who has sown into this congregation and the atmosphere of our church in a deeply personal way, thank you from my heart and from everyone at Deeper Fellowship Church. The seeds you've sown into us are producing a harvest.

Marcos Perez, we never could have known all those years ago that this is why God connected us, but He did, and it's marvelous.

And again to Jason McMullen, this is another part of this unfolding destiny. I'm so happy to be able to work with you on this too!

Finally, Lord, I'm grateful that You would trust me to be one of the stewards of Your move in the earth. My prayer is that my life and these words honor You and bring You glory.

PROLOGUE

Father, You've been present in my life in such an amazing way, and it is mind-blowing to me that You continue to show me Your favor. I pray that Your grace will continue and extend in such a way that Your tangible presence will be felt on every page of this book.

What an amazing God You are that You would desire to dwell among Your people, that You would bless us with the fire of revival, that You would not stay distant and far off. I am undone with the knowledge that, from the foundations of the world, You would create an opportunity for us to get back in right relationship with You so that You can come and be with us.

The potential for what You will do when we surrender and ask blows my mind. You leave me speechless. I am in awe. My breath is taken away by Your glorious presence and power.

Lord, cause Your people to be sensitive to what You want to do and say through me and the words in this book. I don't want to say more than what You're saying; I don't want to do more than what You are doing. I only want to do and say what You are doing and saying. So make us sensitive.

Now, Lord, "let the words of my mouth, and the meditation of my heart, be acceptable in thy sight, O Lord, my strength, and my redeemer" (Ps. 19:14, KJV).

You get the glory. Save us. Visit us. Dwell among us. Revive us. In Jesus's name, amen.

WHAT'S HAPPENING?

Jesus told them, "Go back to John and tell him what you have heard and seen—the blind see, the lame walk, those with leprosy are cured, the deaf hear, the dead are raised to life, and the Good News is being preached to the poor." And he added, "God blesses those who do not fall away because of me."

—MATTHEW 11:4-6

I'T'S HAPPENING! *WHAT'S* happening? Something undeniable is stirring in the church. The global body of Christ is talking about the same thing right now. No matter where you go, you cannot escape hearing the word *revival*. I know it may feel like a Christian buzzword because of how we've used it to describe some of our services and gatherings: "We're going to have a one- (or two- or three-) week revival." But I'm not just referring to a temporary series of good services. I'm talking about the legitimate outpouring of the Holy Spirit that many of us have longed to see.

Revival is here, and I assure you *revival* is not a buzzword. There are people who have gone before us who have prayed and cried and given their lives in intercession for you and me to experience the move of God they never were able to see. And I am here to tell you, it's happening. We've entered into a special time, an amazing season of open heaven, a season that can be defined not by cliché or title but by reality. A season of revival is upon us.

If I were to define *revival* as the outpouring of the Spirit of God in a place or region, then I can tell you that the things that have happened at our church, Deeper Fellowship in Orlando, Florida, since May 22, 2016, bear hallmarks of every historic revival that has taken place in the past four hundred years. There have been salvations,

1

miraculous healings, and a deep awareness that God is in our midst. Even if you've never been to our church, you should get excited about this because this revival is not limited to our church—it is available to everyone. If it's happening anywhere, it can happen everywhere! You too can encounter Him—and you can be a catalyst for revival.

It can be hard to believe that what so many have longed and prayed for is actually here. That's why Matthew 11:4–6, quoted at the opening of this introduction, is an important encouragement for us to hold on to. In this passage John the Baptist, the prophetic forerunner announcing the message of the kingdom and the arrival of the kingdom man, Jesus, found himself in prison at the hands of King Herod. Scripture says when he was in prison, John heard about the works of Christ, so he sent two of his disciples to ask Jesus, "Are You the Messiah we've been expecting, or should we keep looking for someone else?"

What an interesting question when you consider who asked it. John the Baptist was the baby who leaped inside the womb of his mother, Elizabeth, when Mary came to visit while she was pregnant with Jesus. He was the one in the wilderness preaching, "Repent, for the kingdom of heaven is at hand" (Matt. 3:2, MEV). He was the one of whom Jesus said there was no greater prophet. John was the one baptizing people and proclaiming that one greater than he was coming and that he was not even worthy to untie His sandals. John was the one who recognized Jesus and said, "Look! The Lamb of God who takes away the sin of the world!" (John 1:29).

When Jesus came to the Jordan River to be baptized, John tried to prohibit Him, saying, "I need to be baptized by you, and do you come to me?" (Matt. 3:14, NIV). But Jesus told him, "Let it be so now; it is proper for us to do this to fulfill all righteousness" (v. 15, NIV). Only then did John consent. So John also was there when the Spirit descended like a dove and rested on Jesus, and a voice came from heaven saying, "This is my beloved Son, in whom I am well pleased" (Matt. 3:17, KJV).

John the Baptist, the great prophet, preacher, and baptizer, is the one who wanted his disciples to ask Jesus, "Are You the One, or should we look for another?" Perhaps as he was sitting in that prison, some doubts began to fill his mind. Maybe he began wondering, "Is this what life would be like if the Messiah were truly here?" Maybe he thought things would be different. Perhaps that's how we are when we hear about a move of God happening somewhere. We wonder, "Is it possible that this is revival, or should we look somewhere else?" Maybe revival doesn't look the way we thought it would or isn't happening where or how we thought it would take place.

I love how Jesus answered the question John had his disciples ask. Jesus could have simply said, "Yes, I am the Messiah." But He didn't do that. The way Jesus chose to respond would not only answer John but reverberate through all of time.

> Jesus told them, "Go back to John and tell him what you have heard and seen—the blind see, the lame walk, those with leprosy are cured, the deaf hear, the dead are raised to life, and the Good News is being preached to the poor." And he added, "God blesses those who do not fall away because of me."
>
> —Matthew 11:4–6

Basically Jesus was saying, "Go back and tell John it's happening. Tell John that what he'd been prophesying, believing, and praying for—the very reason for his call—is happening." John never got out of the prison, but he did get out of that prison of doubt. He knew from that moment on, it's happening. And Jesus knew that the same thing that would speak to and encourage John would speak to and encourage us: if it's happening anywhere, it can happen everywhere. Said another way, once it's happening anywhere, it's available everywhere.

Many times when the American church starts to talk about moves of God, we point to the mass salvations and innumerable miracles that happen in South America, West Africa, and Western Europe and lament that those things aren't happening in abundance here. However, whenever you hear about a move of God anywhere, that's the time to get excited because it's an indication that the same thing is available to anyone who will posture himself to receive it.

Miracles are breaking out. Undeniable encounters with God are taking place. The presence of God is being tangibly felt. The power of God is present. The people of God are passionately pursuing Him. It's happening!

LET THE RIVERS OF GOD FLOW

I initially did not want to call what we had begun to witness and experience a revival because I didn't want to brand or market a cluster of services as such a divine moment. Everything we have experienced we carry with reverence and honor because we recognize we have not done anything to bring it. But we could do something that causes it to leave. We are recipients of what some theologians call the scandal of particularity, which is all about God asserting His sovereign decision to reveal Himself in a place or to a people simply because He wants to. The only thing we can say about what's happening among us specifically is that God made a sovereign decision to show us favor.

Yet we hold an awareness that like the sensitivity of the Spirit of God, revival can go as suddenly as it came. Our respect for this season, or lack thereof, can sustain or repel the move of God, so we've been very careful to carry it with reverential fear. For this reason we renamed our services "rivers." Based on the truth that everything we do should follow God's leading, we have submitted our services to the flow of what He is doing. We do not control the moments. We do not determine how everything will go.

This setup may not work for everyone. We live in a society that sorely longs to be in control of everything. It's so easy to try to control God or micromanage what we think He can do down to the smallest detail. Across the country, in almost every church in America, we've become really good at attempting to manage the flow of God. We've become really good at programming church to the point that we plan months ahead the experience people are going to have with each clever sermon series and corresponding worship set.

Please understand, I am not against systems or systematic thinking—not at all. What I am against is anything that presupposes that we can control God, because He cannot be controlled. We've learned that in the river of God there cannot be boats with oars. In order to be in the river of God, we must throw down our oars and put up our sails!

The whole point of a revival is for the church to be awakened to the reality, presence, and power of God and for our hearts to be turned to Him. There are people—it might start as a remnant people—who are saying: "Jesus, we want You more than we want anything else. We don't want programs. We want You. And we'll stay as long as it takes. We'll get as loud as we need to get. We'll get on our faces. We'll cry out and let our tears water the seed that we have sown." We will see this revival because it is a revival of people who want Jesus.

One of the greatest tragedies that could ever exist is that the prayers of the saints who have gone before us and who cried and cried out for revival be wasted on a complacent and comfortable church.

One of the greatest tragedies that could ever exist is that the prayers of the saints who have gone before us and who cried and cried out for revival be wasted on a complacent and comfortable church. Many, I'm sure, cried out for things yet not seen that we have the opportunity to see. We must resist the notion to become a "What can You do for me?" church and lean in to what it takes to be passionately on fire for God and filled with His presence to the point that it overflows and affects people everywhere we go. We must refuse to miss this moment.

As of the writing of this book, Deeper Fellowship has been experiencing a tremendous move of God for more than a year. We have seen more than two hundred miracles of physical healing in addition to deliverance, supernatural breakthrough, and salvation. We've begun to grow quite a collection at our altar of unusable crutches, wheelchairs, and other medical devices because people are being healed at each river.

We've never had a so-called "healing service." We have prayed for some people, but many were healed just by being in the presence of God. Some of the miracles we've seen have boggled the minds of medical experts around the country and have set historical records. We've seen cancer healed, tumors disappear, and the effects of strokes reversed. Wheelchairs have been emptied, walkers discarded, deaf ears opened, blindness reversed, rheumatoid arthritis healed, lupus healed multiple times, and carpal tunnel syndrome healed. I was even healed of gout.

One lady in our church, Ms. Pam, used to be partially paralyzed due to a stroke and needed a walker. Now she jumps up and down at the front of the platform during worship! We've seen a partially brain dead baby who doctors said would never smile, talk, or eat on her own instantly healed. One of the most amazing testimonies, or what we call "stories of the river," is when our executive pastor's wife and seven of their nine children were healed of a brain-eating amoeba. I'll share more about that later in this book. All I can tell you is it's happening!

Every time I sit down to write about what God has done, more miracles have happened. There are so many testimonies it's just impossible for me to include them all. That's why the title of this book is *It's Happening* and not *It Happened*, because the stories of the river just keep flowing. We marvel at what we've seen God do. Some of our members had never experienced or been part of a move of God like this before. There's been such a level of awe. We are astounded. And we want more.

A LONG TIME COMING

What God is doing in our midst has been a long time coming. I began to experience this hunger for revival back in 1998 after my pastor at the time suggested that I read Tommy Tenney's book *The God Chasers*. After reading the first chapter or two, I put the book down, went to my room, and began to cry out to God to have an encounter with Him— and I wasn't going to leave until I had one! From that moment on I earnestly cried out for revival to break out somewhere I was. I wanted to see it. I wanted to be there. I wanted to experience it. I wanted to have that kind of encounter with God, and I was desperate to get it. I prayed and cried, and cried and prayed, but I wasn't seeing it.

I would go to church with what I'll call a frustrated anticipation. I lived with the expectation that any service could be *the* service where it would happen. I prayed for it, and I constantly looked for it. I'd see a couple of on-fire people here or there, but there never seemed to be an entire church that pursued God and didn't care what time the service let out. In the prayer gatherings held at my mom's house, where I stayed at the time, I would see glimpses of what could be. A group of friends would come over with no agenda but to seek God. At those gatherings we sought God intensely. Incidentally it was during those times of worship and prayer that my sensitivity to the voice of God grew and I learned how to host His presence. My longing led me through lonely times, isolation, ridicule, and being called weird. Still I prayed because I was determined to see revival.

I didn't recognize that my prayers were setting me up for my life. I also didn't realize that when I was asking God to bring forth a generation that wanted revival as badly as I did, He would lead me into covenant with the members at Deeper. Fast-forward twenty years, and now Deeper is three years old publicly and six years old for those of us who've been part of the core group. For the first three years we met as a small group in my living room. Throughout those first three years we had one specific prayer: we wanted to see a move of God. Our first official act as a group was to take a map of the city of Orlando and put our tears on it. I still have that map at my house. We wept over our city and asked God for revival. God heard our cries, and He is responding. When I cry now, my tears often come because I am beginning to see what I have prayed for. It's happening! Since May 22, 2016, we've used that phrase as an encouragement to one another, recognizing that God is doing what He said He would do.

GET YOUR HOPES UP

After not seeing God move mightily in the church in America for so long, the door of disappointment has been opened, and a spirit of skepticism has entered. It has changed our faith-filled speech to doubt-filled discourse. Our spirits bear witness to this defeating spirit that causes us to say, "Don't get my hopes up. Don't talk to me about my dreams. Don't talk to me about my potential. I've made peace with disappointment." But that is exactly what the word of the Lord comes to do. The word of the Lord comes to awaken the hope inside you to cause you to fall out of agreement with disappointment and align with hope. Your days of disappointment are over; your season of manifestation is here.

Perhaps you were once active in your local church, serving on the worship team and maybe the prayer team. Maybe you were part of groups that prayed for the move of God to come to your church or city, but after years of praying, it seemed nothing was happening. Maybe you cried out before God in the privacy of your home, where no one else could see. What if I told you that not one word of your prayers and not one tear from your eyes went without response? The seeds you've sown in the past are going to manifest now. You are going to receive a harvest for seeds you have forgotten you have sown.

If you had been praying before but stopped, I want to encourage you to do it again. Maybe you've fasted already. Do it again. You've already walked the floor at night, contending with God for a visitation. Do it again. I know you've cried already. Do it again. Why? Because revival didn't happen the first time.

We live in a generation whose mantra is "If at first you don't succeed, give up and try it a different way." It doesn't work that way with God. God answers persistence. Some of you have given up because the revival didn't happen when you thought it should have. But what if you gave up too soon?

God is looking for people who have a persistent faith, an unwavering, unshakable faith; people who will say to God, "You did it before; You can do it again." There is a revival coming to the United States of America. I've seen it. We are in a season of manifestation, and it is going to be attached to those who are willing to do whatever God requires again and again and again until something happens!

LEAVING ROOM FOR RESPONSE

One of the things that I think are important in considering an atmosphere that is ripe for revival is our response to what God is doing. How we respond to God is connected to the results we receive while He is near. In 2 Kings 6 and 7 there was a great famine in Samaria, and Elisha prophesied its sudden end. But the officer assisting the king resisted the word, saying the famine couldn't end as Elisha said even if God opened the windows of heaven. Well, the next day everything Elisha prophesied came to pass. The king's officer saw it happen, but he didn't experience it, all because he didn't believe the word and act accordingly.

Our response to the word of the Lord determines our experience and results. At the end of each chapter in this book I have created an invitation for you to look into your heart and see what you need to do to be in the right posture to receive what God is wanting to do in the earth in this season. I am calling it "Respond."

Your response to the word of the Lord determines your results.

In this section you may be led to pray, search your heart, or take some other action. God is calling you out of your comfort zone, out of yourself and your comforts, out of the norm. Your response to Him determines how He will respond in your home, your community, the nation, and the world. It is an exchange: we pray; God responds. Our response to God determines what we will experience.

WILL YOU JOIN US?

On the Friday night after our church's dramatic encounter with the Lord on May 22, 2016, I was ministering to our young adults when I realized I was entering the middle of my life and I had been praying for a move of God for almost half of my life. Now that we are seeing it manifest, I am not going to waste time doing programmed and predictable church. I am going to water that seed with my tears. I want to see a revival hit this nation, not just my church, and I don't care how much the best church-growth strategists say people won't come. I'm not moved by how many people come to Deeper or how long our services last. We stay until He's finished.

The multitudes would stay all day with Jesus because things happened in His presence. I don't know about you, but I know I need Him. I want Him. And I will not stop until I see revival across the nation and around the world. I am going to weep for it, cry out for it, pray for it, fast for it, wait for it, and live in anticipation of it. What are you willing to do to see it come?

People will talk about you and make fun of you. That's OK. They are going to say you're weird and crazy. That's OK. You know why? Because they need revival. They are just not willing to do whatever it takes to get it. But if they stay around you long enough, they will ride on your coattails, and that's OK. Some of us want Him; all of us need Him. Revival does not need everyone for it to spread. Just a remnant crying out for God will get heaven's attention.

God assembled Deeper, bringing us together for a divine purpose, and now He has released something through our little corner warehouse church. People stand in line outside to get in. Why? Because they know it's happening. And now that it's happened with us, we are believing the fire will spread to you.

It's happening. And if it's happening anywhere, it can happen everywhere!

CHAPTER 1

WHEN HE WALKED INTO THE ROOM

> At the sound of Mary's greeting, Elizabeth's child leaped within her, and Elizabeth was filled with the Holy Spirit. Elizabeth gave a glad cry and exclaimed to Mary…"When I heard your greeting, the baby in my womb jumped for joy. You are blessed because you believed that the Lord would do what he said."
>
> **—LUKE 1:41–45**

I WRITE DOWN MANY of the things the Lord has done in our midst, just for the sake of memory. One day as I was writing some things down, the presence of the Lord began to fill the room. I was overwhelmed and unable to keep my composure as I thought about all I have seen. What is happening in this season is precious. God is giving us a moment, an opportunity, an invitation to experience and encounter Him—to go all in. The Lord wants to do something greater than anything we've experienced before. Can you imagine what would happen if we gave Him room to do it?

I have been on a search for something nearly my entire life. I grew up in church. I was the kid who played church at home. At first, it was the music that kept me interested because I was a very musical child. I still am very musical. In fact, most people first encountered my ministry through my worship leading. The music was so good at my church that I actually didn't want to go to children's church when I was a little kid. In those days children's church was basically something to keep us occupied until we got old enough for the adult service. That was where it was happening. Back then gospel recording artist Donald Lawrence was our minister of music. If you are familiar with his ministry, then you can see why I wanted to be with the adults.

By the time I was nine or ten years old, it wasn't only the music that kept my attention. I also started listening to the messages. I started to feel as if there was more to this church thing than good music. You may wonder how a ten-year-old would think like this, but it was the Holy Spirit planting a seed in my spirit. I had no frame of reference to know there was something more. I just knew there was.

When I was ten years old, my mother went on a business trip to Los Angeles and came back filled with the Holy Spirit. She visited Crenshaw Christian Center and was exposed to things we had never experienced. We were Baptist, and supernatural stuff such as healing, the gifts of the Spirit, and signs and wonders wasn't really discussed at our church. Now, don't get me wrong; the gospel was preached, and people were getting saved. But there is more to our spiritual existence, and even at ten years old I was getting hungry for it.

The next time my mother went to California, she took me with her. It was my spring break, and we had a full itinerary—Disneyland, Knott's Berry Farm, Universal Studios, and some other must-see places. We had great fun. But she also made sure to take me to the church where she had received the baptism of the Holy Spirit. I saw things I had never seen before. I heard things I had never heard before. I saw people encounter God and become weak and unable to stand because of the weight of His presence—what some believers call being "slain in the Spirit." On one side of the room people were being prayed for, and on the other side of the room people were falling down because they could feel what was happening on the other side of the room. You can imagine that as a ten-year-old I was scared to death.

I heard people speaking and singing in other languages and in unknown tongues. That scared me too, but I wanted it.

Then someone said, "We're going to pray for healing, so if you're sick in your body, come up." At that time I dealt with really bad asthma. I had even been hospitalized once. My mother, who served on the board of the American Lung Association of Southwest Ohio, had been putting all her efforts into finding a cure for it. So she said, "Go up there. Go."

But after all I had seen at the church that day—people falling out for what I thought was no reason—I thought, "No way." Then I saw that she was crying. Through her tears she said, "I believe that if you'll just go, you'll be healed." Literally weeping, she pleaded again, "Please. Go."

Understand that this was happening in the 1980s, before Christian TV was as widespread as it is today, so not many people were exposed to this kind of thing. This was unfamiliar territory for me.

It was a midweek service. I remember going up for prayer, but I don't actually remember what happened after that. I do know this: I don't suffer from asthma anymore. We went back on Sunday, and I had to go to children's church there because they didn't allow children in the main service. However, I was filled with the Holy Spirit in their children's church. After spending one week in California and attending two church services, I had experienced the presence of God in a brand-new way, and I was marked for life. Since that time when I was ten, I have not been the same.

BECOMING A GOD CHASER

Two years later we found ourselves in a church where there was a full-on outpouring of the Holy Spirit. People would stand outside in line for more than an hour in sub-zero temperatures, waiting to get in. Why? Because God was there. But after a while people became comfortable and complacent. If we aren't intentional, we can easily lose our awe of God and set up camp in the land of comfort. Whenever this happens, whenever we take the move of God for granted, things will change. Eventually our church went back to normal. But the hunger and fire in me continued to burn.

Several years later a pastor and mentor of mine came up to me and said, "Hey, why don't you read this book?" He was holding a copy of *The God Chasers* by Tommy Tenney. The message and testimonies in that book moved me from saying, "I want that," to being obsessed with possessing the kingdom. I longed to know and be known by God and to pursue Him until I experienced Him in a profound and tangible way. He was who I wanted.

I've had moments in my life when I've seen God move, but they were fleeting. I've been in services where His presence was intense, but eventually things returned to normal, as if the amazing service didn't even happen. I've been at restaurants where a simple conversation turned into a deep awareness of God's presence because He sat down in the booth with us. But the people in those restaurants went back to normal, and their fire seemed to be extinguished. I've been with friends, preparing to eat a meal, and the blessing turned into a God encounter that left us all on the floor before God. As a worship leader, I've led worship during times when no one knew what to say or do because we all were arrested by the presence of God. I've also seen moments like those dishonored because something else was on a program.

Have you experienced what I'm talking about? If so, do you still cry out? Do you still burn for God? Do you still want Him more than anything? I know I do.

I have never lost my cry. We planted our church with this cry. We want to see a move of God. We want to see it grow beyond the seven hundred to eight hundred people who gather together in a corner warehouse. We want to see it spread to our city, state, nation, and world. God is moving powerfully among us. He is moving in you. Do you want more?

THE DAY MY BABY LEAPED

There are many different ways people become aware that God is planning to visit His church. The great revivalists and prophets of old had visions, dreams, and angelic visitations that let them know God was near. That's not what happened with me. I felt my baby leap.

It was 2001, a couple of years after I had read *The God Chasers*. At that time I was traveling as the music director and keyboardist for worship leader Ron Kenoly. We were ministering in South

Bend, Indiana, at the church Lester Sumrall once pastored. I don't remember anything specific about the service that night, but what God did in me after our time of ministry I will remember for the rest of my life.

Before the night of worship began, I had a conversation with Lester Sumrall's grandson. I remember us talking about the move of God we wanted to see in our generation. After the night of worship was over, we were standing in the parking lot, continuing to talk about the future move of God we were so desperate to see. As we were talking, I felt the strangest sensation. I physically felt something move inside of me. I had never felt anything like it in my entire life, and honestly it startled me. What happened next startled me even more. The person I was talking with said, "Dude, did you feel that?"

"Feel what?" I said, even though I had felt something. He said, "Did your baby just leap?" I had never felt anything like it in my life, but in that moment I knew that's what had just happened, so I had to acknowledge it.

I've not birthed any babies, obviously, but there is no other way to describe the leap I felt in my body that day. The Bible indicates that this leaping is symbolic of God's confirming that He hears our prayers and is answering them.

In Luke 1 Gabriel went to Zechariah and said, "God has heard your prayer" (v. 13). His prayer was for a child. Zechariah and Elizabeth were barren, and they were old. But God gave them John the Baptist, who was filled with the Holy Spirit in the womb and became a forerunner of Christ.

Six months into Elizabeth's pregnancy Gabriel appeared to Mary and announced that she had been chosen to carry the Messiah. Mary and Elizabeth were relatives, and a few days after her angelic visitation, Mary went to visit Elizabeth. As they greeted each other, the Bible says the baby inside Elizabeth leaped for joy. After coming in contact with Jesus, after coming in contact with what was on the inside of Mary, John leaped, as if he were saying, "My reason for living has just arrived."

This is what happened to my friend and me that day. Jesus walked into our conversation and confirmed to us that we were going in the right direction toward our purpose, toward having our hunger for Him satisfied and our thirst quenched. Just as it was with Elizabeth, my baby leaped when Jesus walked in. The desire God placed in me as a ten-year-old was alive. That leaping sensation was an announcement from heaven that God was coming to dwell among us—that I would see what I had been praying for.

My entire life has been lived to intentionally position myself for the day when God would walk in the room. Every service I led, every sermon I preached, every song I sang anywhere in the world was in anticipation of the moment God Himself would come and visit with us. The only thing I asked was, "God, let me be there. Let me see it. Let me be in the room when it happens." And He answered my prayer on May 22, 2016.

THE DAY *IT* HAPPENED

It was a Sunday morning, and I woke up between 5:30 and 6:00, as I did every Sunday, to pray and spend time with the Lord to prepare my spirit for the day. I always look forward to our worship gatherings because our church is filled with people who are pursuing an encounter with God. The service began like most others, but during the worship I began to feel unease in my spirit. It wasn't because something was wrong. I just had a sense that something more was supposed to happen, but I didn't know what.

I preached the message God had given me, but even when the service was over, I still had that uneasy feeling, and I didn't know why. Uneasy is the best way I can describe it. It felt like a mixture of nervous energy, anticipation of the unknown, and uncertainty about what to do next. We have two services, which we call River 1 and River 2, and between the two I remember saying to my best friend Caleb, who is the associate pastor at Deeper, "I feel like God wants to do more or say something different from what I preached, and I'm not sure what it is yet." I asked him to handle the transition to the second service so I could press in to God to see what He wanted to do. As we began to worship for River 2, that uneasy feeling would not leave me. In fact, it intensified. The closer it came to my time to preach, the more intense the feeling became. But I still did not have a sense of what God wanted me to say or do.

Then, right before I got up to speak, it happened. The baby leaped again! I experienced the exact sensation I had felt sixteen years earlier. I hadn't experienced anything like it since that day in South Bend, but there it was. Suddenly I began to weep uncontrollably. As I stood in front of the entire congregation weeping, I thought I should attempt to explain what I'd just felt, knowing how foolish it would sound for a man to explain to everyone that his baby had just leaped. Through my tears I tried my best to tell them what had happened sixteen years earlier, and while I was talking, other people began to weep. My friend Caleb, who knew what had happened to me sixteen years before, looked at me from the front row and said, "It's happening."

What happened next is hard to fully explain. What began with me weeping uncontrollably suddenly swept through the entire room. Without prompting or a single word spoken, people began to rush to the front of the church, falling on their knees, weeping and crying out to God. It wasn't just a few; it was the majority of the room. Nobody gave an altar call. There was no human catalyst to prompt that moment. It wasn't a response to what I preached because I couldn't even speak. It wasn't a response to a song because nothing was being sung at the time. The Lord walked into the room, and everyone knew it at the same time. Everyone felt it at the same time. Everyone was aware, and no one could do anything but weep.

We stayed there and wept in the presence of God for literally hours. The service that began at 11:30 a.m. continued until 3:30 p.m. officially, but people stayed beyond that time. I remember thinking at one point while I was there crying that none of the first-time visitors would ever come back. Imagine the story afterward.

"So how was Deeper Fellowship?"

"Well, the pastor got up and said he could feel a baby inside of him, and then he started crying, and then everyone started crying, and they kept crying for hours."

I thought, "What must those who have yet to surrender their lives to Christ be thinking?" The pastor part of me was thinking those things, but the one who had been crying out for this my entire life couldn't stop the moment. Being concerned in the back of my mind about what people would think almost caused me to make a huge mistake.

Genuine encounters with God change you.

I looked at the clock and decided to give those who wanted to leave a safe exit. I stood up and gave a soft dismissal, but I didn't offer an invitation for salvation. Immediately the Holy Spirit convicted me and reminded me about the Day of Pentecost in Acts chapter 2, when the promised Holy Spirit came. You can imagine the many things that must have been happening when the sound of a mighty windstorm could be heard throughout the room and what looked like tongues of fire appeared and people began to speak in other languages. Some thought they were drunk. Scripture says Peter gave prophetic context to what was happening, and that day three thousand people went from confusion to conversion.

As some people were leaving, I stood up and said, "Wait! If you have been here this entire time and haven't left, it is because you are clearly looking for Christ, and He is here now. If you want to surrender to Him, now is your opportunity." To my surprise people literally began to run to the front of the church to surrender to Christ. A service with no preaching that had gone on for hours with uncontrollable weeping left numerous people saying, "I want in on this."

That was the day everything changed for me and for our church. What we experienced wasn't a one-time occurrence but rather a life-altering change. It's hard to prove biblically that you've had an encounter with God without change. Genuine encounters with God change you. When I went home that day, I didn't even want to speak. I didn't want to do anything that would cause my awareness of Him and His nearness to change.

I called my friend Caleb the next day because I could still tangibly feel the presence of God, and when he answered, he was still in that place as well. All we could do on the phone was weep. As I am writing this now, I've had to stop and weep. It was such a holy moment that even talking about it brings me right back to that experience.

I spent that entire week essentially in a place of solitude and reverence because of our encounter. The following Friday I was scheduled to minister to our young adults, and as I went to prepare my notes, once again I began to weep uncontrollably in my home. I fell to my knees in worship with the keen awareness that God likely wasn't going to use my notes. The Lord spoke to me and said He was going to show up during the service. My only instruction was to talk until He came. After the icebreaker and the time of worship was complete, I sat on a chair in front of our young adults, knowing what the Lord had spoken to me but not knowing how or when He would come, so I just started talking.

I started sharing my journey with God and part of my testimony, and then suddenly it happened. He came, and we all knew it at the same time. We began to weep and worship. This went on for hours. I remember thinking, "There is nothing else for me to say or do." The very presence of the Lord was there. We laugh about it today, but I attempted to give the service over to my friend Caleb, who also happens to be the young adults pastor. Yet through his weeping— the most tears you can imagine someone having—he strained to say, "I can't!" He was literally unable to do anything but weep. I understood because that's exactly how I and everyone else in the room were feeling. We were unable to speak or sing or do anything but weep because of the presence of the Lord. The young adults service, which began at 7:30 p.m., ended at 3:30 a.m. During the eight hours we spent in the presence of the Lord, it felt as if time were suspended. We've never been the same since. We refuse to go back to the way life was before.

My pastor, Bishop Joseph Garlington, had visited our church pre-viously and prophesied to us that divine interruptions were coming. So *it*—the outpouring of the Holy Spirit, the divine interruption, the divine invitation—happened. The opening of the floodgates, the realization of an open heaven, the discovery of our cry, the reason for our tears—it happened. God made an announcement to us. He confirmed that it's alive—what He placed in me, in us, and in you is alive. Do you know what they call it? Revival.

SIGNS OF REVIVAL

Since that day I have been researching revivals that have broken out over the last four centuries. I've done this for several reasons. There's a part of our church culture in the West that causes us to want to brand a string of good services as "revival." Because what God did was so sudden, I wanted to make sure we didn't prematurely call what we were seeing revival. As a result, we began to say, "It's hap-pening." And it was and is.

But I discovered something more. As of this moment every sign I have read about that marked the revivals that have taken place in the last four centuries—salvation, repentance, healings—has happened and is happening in our church. The only exception is we have not seen the effects on social systems in the area that marked the Welsh revival—lowered crime rates, fewer police officers, increased eco-nomic status, and the like. God is big, and He's just getting started, so I won't rule that out. Yet and still, outside of the Welsh Revival every other historic revival in the last four centuries has included what we are seeing.

This is revival.

You may not have been at my church the day "it" happened. Most likely you weren't there, because only a few hundred of us were in the room. But the thing I've learned about revival, which I will share more about later, is that if God is doing something anywhere in the world, the heavens are ripe for Him to do it everywhere. What He is doing for us He will do for you—He may have already started doing it. When God pours out His Spirit, the experience is not exclusive. Joel 2:28 says He will pour His Spirit out on all flesh. So I challenge you to allow that old desire for more of God to come alive again. Let the hope of a fresh outpouring for all nations and people come alive in you again.

The thing I've learned about revival is that if God is doing something anywhere in the world, the heavens are ripe for Him to do it everywhere. What He is doing for us He will do for you.

We never could have calculated when God would literally walk in the room and sit with us. We never could have prepared ourselves for that moment. But we were empty containers. We held on to the prayers of those who had died without seeing what they had prayed for come to pass. We hoped against hope, and hope did not disappoint. He gave us the desire of our hearts. He gave us Himself. Now we contend for the atmosphere to remain open and receptive to His presence. And He has been teaching us what it will take to see that happen.

RESPOND

I have a question for you: What is all this worth to you—the presence, revival, God's power demonstrated, His blessings manifested, the outpouring of His Spirit? What are the hundreds of years of people crying day after day and night after night for revival, yet never seeing it come to pass, worth to you? Is it worth enough for you to go after it? I am going to level with you: pursuing God is an inconvenient, uncomfortable mission, but it is a priceless, eternal possession when you attain it, like the treasure hidden in the field. (See Matthew 13:44–46.) The man in that parable sold everything he owned to get enough money to buy the field—that's how valuable the treasure was to him.

We're being invited to take a risk to buy the field with the buried treasure. Not everybody will go in on this one. There are a whole lot of people who have decided revival costs too much, and they are unwilling to go through what it takes and give up everything to possess it. Maybe you want to bargain as the rich young ruler did in Matthew 19:16–30. Maybe you want to see how you can keep everything you have and get God. Jesus says you can't.

God requires everything, and His movement in our lives depends on our level of surrender and our capacity to be filled with His Spirit. Giving up everything leaves room for the greatest amount of His power to become active in your life. What is that worth to you?

If you want to see and be part of the next greatest move of God and you want it so badly that you are willing to do whatever it takes to see it, I invite you to pray this prayer with me:

> *Father, give me the courage to buy the field. There's a treasure in it, and I want it. I want what You have for me, my family, my church, my city, and my nation. I release everything to You that is holding me back from seeing You move. The treasure I seek is You, and nothing else will satisfy me. Come, Lord Jesus. Amen.*

CHAPTER 2

HOW'S YOUR POSTURE?

S INCE GOD WALKED in, all we've wanted to do is maintain the right position to keep Him here. We call it posture. Posture is the attitude—mental or spiritual—people develop, usually in response to how external forces affect their internal world.

When I was growing up, my mom, my aunts, church mothers, and other elders were always telling us kids, "Fix your posture." They knew the deal. Posture is attitude. You know grown folks don't like when young people have attitudes. Posture is about disposition.

What is your posture before God? What is your spiritual attitude? My posture before the Lord is waiting. My posture before the Lord is honor. My posture before the Lord is crying out to Him. My posture before the Lord is making room for Him. All these things communicate to God that we respond to His invitation with an eternal yes and eagerly anticipate what He wants to release in the earth.

Now, before we go further, there's something I need to clarify: posture is not about working for the blessing of God or working to make something happen. We don't have to do that. God shows up in encounters of His choosing, not ours. By definition an encounter is a surprise or unexpected meeting. In other words, it's planned by someone else. All we can do is continue to position ourselves for encounters with God. If we do try to make something happen, we'll look up one day and find ourselves talking about what *was* instead of what *is*, trying to carry something emotionally and in our own strength because God is not breathing on it. The Lord is inviting us to a place where we can partner with Him and what He wants to do in our homes, our churches and cities, our nation, and the world. He is just looking for people who have the right posture.

There are nine postures the Lord revealed to us in the early days of His movement. Many of these will be discussed throughout the book, so I will introduce them only briefly. But they will be here for you to see all in one place, and you can come back to them as many times as you need to as the Lord increases your hunger for Him.

1. WAITING

In Acts 1:4–5 Jesus told His followers, "Do not leave Jerusalem until the Father sends you the gift he promised, as I told you before. John baptized with water, but in just a few days you will be baptized with the Holy Spirit." Most teach from the perspective that there were only 120 people in this group, but a further look tells us there were actually five hundred. (See Matthew 28:18–20; 1 Corinthians 15:6.) At the time when the Holy Spirit came in like a rushing wind (Acts 2:2), there were only the 120. What happened to the other 380?

Some of us rebuke the devil when it's not the devil at all. It's God using that circumstance to cause us to seek Him.

Anything could have caused them to change their posture from the "stay and wait" position in which Jesus asked them to remain. Those who stayed received the promise. They refused to settle for a secondhand experience. They waited until they saw what had been promised. They took the posture of "God, I'm not leaving until…"

2. DESPERATION

This posture can show up in two ways: divine desperation and desperation by frustration. The difference between divine desperation and desperation by frustration is the recognition of one's need for God. Each of these postures of desperation will lead you to a different place. Desperation by frustration is birthed out of exasperation or frustration and will lead you to do anything in search of relief, even if what you do is without God. This posture is best seen in the life of King Saul. (See 1 Samuel 28.) After the prophet Samuel died, Saul was no longer able to hear from God since he had never developed a prophetic relationship with Him. The Philistine army was forming against Israel, and Saul was desperate for a word, so he sought out the witch of Endor. His actions led to the kingdom being stripped from him and his murder.

The posture of divine desperation, on the other hand, leads you to a fuller awareness of your need for God. This desperation comes from God. He places longings, and sometimes circumstances or situations, in our lives that cause us to seek Him. There are some of us who rebuke the devil when it's not the devil at all. It's God using that circumstance to cause us to seek Him. In Jeremiah 29:4–12 we see where the Lord orchestrated the events surrounding Israel's seventy-year Babylonian captivity to cause them to seek and desire Him once again. He led them into a desperate circumstance, but He also promised that when they recognized their need for Him again, He would hear their prayers and deliver them.

3. Crying

God is looking for a people who will literally cry out to Him and allow their tears to water their spiritual seed so the harvest can come. The story of Jacob paints a good picture of how a posture of crying will position you for a life-altering encounter with God.

Jacob's story is familiar to many people. He's the one who cried out, "I won't let go until You bless me!" He's the one who wrestled with God and won. But how can a man wrestle pound for pound with God and win? Let's think about that. We can't really wrestle with God and win. I mean, God just took His finger, touched Jacob lightly on the hip, and maimed him for life. We can't wrestle God. The truth is God didn't want Jacob to let Him go. So then how did Jacob get what He wanted? The answer is not found in Genesis 32, where we read of how Jacob wrestled with God. It's found in Hosea 12:4:

> Yes, he wrestled with the angel and won. He wept and pleaded for a blessing from him. There at Bethel he met God face to face, and God spoke to him.

Jacob wrestled with the angel and won because of his tears. Days after the encounter I called Pastor Caleb, and as we talked on the phone, we both began to weep. We could barely speak because the presence of God was overwhelming. That Friday as I prepared for the young adults service, I sat in my room, weeping for two hours. Then that night during the service, God did it again, and the Deeper young adults stayed until 2:30 in the morning, weeping. If you recall the times when you felt God so close, didn't you weep too?

When this happens, we are contending with God. Crying out to God shows that we are no longer trying to figure things out on our own. The only way we're going to see what we've been praying for is if we weep. If we will be a people who will weep, who will cry out to God, I guarantee that we will be at the epicenter of the next revival.

4. PRAYER

Prayer is ultimately a declaration of our dependence on God. It's a dialogue between God and man. It's the reserved seat in the heavenly realms from which we affect things in the earth. Therefore, it is an ideal posture for one who is praying for God to move upon the earth.

What we must be careful of is to not allow our prayers and declarations to become self-centered. Sometimes in the church our beliefs are self-centered, and what we pray about, think about, talk about, and believe God for usually has something to do with us.

But this may be where another posture overlaps: often desperation leads to intercession, where you begin to pray for those who are unaware of their need for God. Your prayers change from "God, I need You" to "God, we need You." Desperate people don't just cry out for themselves. They begin to look at the hopelessness and the state of the world around them, and they begin to say, "God, we need revival."

Prayer is at the center of much of what we do at Deeper. We have a prayer call at 7:00 a.m. and another one at 9:00 p.m. Monday through Friday. Right now there are more than 150 of us who get on that call and assume the posture of prayer. Prayer helps us keep momentum. We all stand on the prayers of past generations. The revivals that break out are a result of past prayers. Our posture of prayer now will keep those prayers alive.

Desperate people don't just cry out for themselves. They begin to look at the hopelessness and the state of the world around them, and they begin to say, "God, we need revival."

When you have experienced a special visitation from God, in order to see that moment turn into something that will outlast you, you must continue to do what got you there. In a later chapter we are going to talk about how to create the window through which God's presence will shower down upon us continually. We will talk about how the Bible instructs us to pray for more rain in the season of rain. Do not let it dry up. Keep praying for God to invade every space and fill us with His presence.

- -

Stories
of the River

During this outpouring the gifts of prophecy, words of knowledge, and words of wisdom have been alive and active in our midst. We fully embrace these gifts and can directly testify to how the Lord has moved time and time again in incredibly accurate ways as a result of these things.

First Corinthians 14:24–25 says: "But if all prophesy and there comes in one who does not believe or one unlearned, he is convinced by all and judged by all. Thus the secrets of his heart are revealed. And so falling down on his face, he will worship God and report that God is truly among you" (MEV). We saw this happen among us one Sunday morning.

I stood up to preach, but the spirit of prophecy was very strong, and many words of knowledge were given and released that day. At one point I specifically heard the Lord say, "Watch for the day of the Walmart miracle." So I told the church, "The Lord says, 'Watch for the day of the Walmart miracle.'" Then I expounded on the word and said that someone was going to go into a Walmart and have a divine encounter.

As I was speaking, a tall, slender gentleman whom I had not previously seen at our church came forward looking as if he had seen a ghost. He had been in Walmart that morning and had encountered one of our faithful members, who invited him and his girlfriend to come to church that morning. He'd had an encounter with God during the service and was weeping uncontrollably.

Caleb, our young adults pastor, then began to prophesy to him, revealing what his life was like in the past and the word of the Lord for his future. This young man surrendered his life to Christ in that moment—and it just so happens that he and his girlfriend were both Muslims. First Corinthians 14:25 happened right then and there. Two people literally fell on their faces, worshipped God, and said by their actions, "God is truly among you." It's happening!

- -

5. WORSHIP

We are in a generation obsessed with gaining knowledge about worship. Today there are likely more books about worship and worship songs than at any other time in history. We know the lingo, we know the stage placement, our musicianship is impeccable, but where are our hearts? Our external expressions in worship should reflect our internal posture; otherwise we are not giving God worship. We're only performing. The acts of worship without repentance—another posture—merely become rituals.

Jesus said it to the woman at the well: there's coming a time when

God will be looking for a people who will be honest with Him. He is not looking for ritual and form. He is looking for the heart.

Our true posture in worship is tested when our humanity encounters God's divinity. Worship acknowledges one greater than we are. Our posture during and after encounters with God reveals much about our hearts. When we don't worship from a place of self-denial, we can become prideful and think we can come up with some formula to invoke God's presence. That's not how worship works. Worship is a pathway, an invitation from God to be positioned for encounters with Him.

Encounters are of His choosing, not ours, but worship positions us for them. God is not in our presence; we are in His presence. This is key to our understanding of the posture of worship. It is an honor to be in the presence of the Lord. When the prophet Isaiah saw the Lord in the year King Uzziah died, he was completely undone by what he experienced. The realization of humanity encountering divinity caused him to say, "Woe is me! For I am undone" (Isa. 6:5, MEV). He immediately recognized his frailty in relation to the holiness of God.

The amazing thing is that God allowed him to experience that vision in order to invite him into His plan. It was a God-given encounter that allowed Isaiah to glimpse the worship happening in heaven. God exposed him to His holiness and majesty and confirmed Isaiah's calling. The posture of worship does the same for us. It exposes us to the divine, causes us to recognize our own human frailty in relation to His holiness, and brings us into a place of revelation.

We must reconnect our external expressions of worship with what's really happening in our hearts. Repentance helps us get there. If we cannot get our hearts and lives in position to give God the worship He is worthy of, then we will miss out on one of the main vehicles of access to Him and His presence.

6. DELIBERATE ACTION

The story of the woman with the issue of blood is a perfect example of how the posture of deliberate action leads to an encounter with God that changes everything. The Bible says in Luke 8:46 that Jesus noticed when someone "deliberately touched" Him. She was not casual about what she needed from God. She had tried everything to be healed. Now penniless and desperate, she heard that Jesus was passing by. She considered her options, she considered her unclean status, and she made a deliberate choice to risk it all and grab hold of His garment.

There are no accidental moves of God. If you are going to experience God, it's not going to happen by being random. If you want a greater demonstration of the power of God in your life, you must deliberately pursue Him. Make the intentional effort to risk it all—reach out and grab hold.

7. FAITH

The Lord asks, "When the Son of Man comes, will he find faith on the earth?" (Luke 18:8, NIV). Or will He return to find a bunch of frustrated believers? Faith is a posture that allows the faithful to endure the tension between present afflictions and future deliverance.

God is looking for people who have a persistent faith—an unwavering, unshakable faith. He is looking for people who, in the midst of waiting, will say to God, "You've done it before; You will do it again."

Faith gives us confidence that what we hope for will happen. It gives us assurance about the things we cannot see. Faith makes us pleasing to God. Faith gives us permission to come to God. God rewards those who sincerely seek Him. Faith makes us whole.

I pray that as you read this book, you will feel a faith arise in you that you haven't felt in a long time. I declare that your capacity to believe God again is being restored. May your faith come to new life as you begin to see what you've been hoping for come to pass.

8. OBEDIENCE

Worship, prayer, sacrifice, giving—what does any of it mean if we won't obey God? Obedience is the posture that God wants most. As a matter of fact, obedience to Him helps us know what He wants us to do with our worship, prayer, sacrifice, and giving. Through our simple obedience to God in whatever He asks, especially the things that seem foolish to our limited understanding, we unlock the deep things, the mysteries we desire to understand. Revival is connected to simple obedience.

King Saul refused to obey the Lord. He refused to assume the posture of obedience, and it cost him dearly. He never saw the things he'd once hoped for happen. For him, *it* never happened. When Saul was coming up against an enemy of the armies of the living God (Israel), God told him to kill and destroy everything. No matter how good something looked, no matter what kind of agreement they were offered, no matter what kind of purse they could receive, they were to "completely destroy the entire Amalekite nation—men, women, children, babies, cattle, sheep, goats, camels, and donkeys" (1 Sam. 15:3).

But Saul spared the enemy King Agag. He also let his soldiers keep the spoils. When God questioned Saul's actions through the prophet Samuel, Saul lied and made it seem as if the spoils were kept to honor God. Samuel said to him, "What is more pleasing to the LORD: your burnt offerings and sacrifices or your obedience to his voice? Listen! Obedience is better than sacrifice, and submission is better than offering the fat of rams....Because you have rejected the command of the LORD, he has rejected you as king" (1 Sam. 15:22–23).

Obedience is an important posture to maintain. It's a posture of surrender and submission to the will and ways of God. It is a demonstration of our eternal yes to God's invitation into His presence. We cannot have God and be disobedient to Him. Disobedience without repentance puts us at risk of losing everything God has for us. I'm not willing to lose Him. I will take whatever posture I have to take to maintain His presence in my life. How about you?

9. REPENTANCE

Repentance is the pathway to revival. It keeps the avenue between us and God open for whenever He decides to come and rest upon our lives. If we are unwilling to let go of the things that block what God wants, we will never see His power on display in the earth. It is

God's gift to us that allows us to stay in His presence. Repentance is a hard practice for this generation to latch on to. We don't like to feel bad about anything. But if we look at it from God's perspective, we will see it as His desire to draw near to us. Repentance draws Him close. And when His holiness enters the room and comes in contact with our unholiness, we think we feel guilt, but it's actually His light illuminating our darkness. All we have to do is get in a posture of repentance. He is faithful and just to forgive us our sins, cleanse us of unrighteousness, and dwell among us. We do not have to run away. He has made a way for us to boldly enter His presence.

God wants to do something great. If you are hungry to see revival, you are ready to do whatever God asks of you to be the vessel through which His glory comes.

RESPOND

It's easy to get excited about revival, but are you willing to assume the right posture to lay hold of it? Are you willing to deliberately reach out and touch Jesus as the woman with the issue of blood did—to touch Him in a way that pulls on His power? Everyone claims to want Him, but will you pray until you touch Him? Will you worship until you touch Him? Will you wait until you touch Him? Will you risk rejection to touch Him? Will you accept ridicule to touch Him?

We're not going to accidentally enter into revival. We'll see it when we're willing to assume the posture that says, "I want You and You alone, and I won't stop praying, I won't stop crying, I won't stop worshipping until You come. And then I'll keep on worshipping and keep on praying and keep on crying because I'm desperate. I want to be a vessel for Your glory. Ordinary won't do. I want to be part of what You're doing in the earth. Revival is here, and I want to be a part of it!" When that is our posture, God will respond.

CHAPTER 3

HE HEARS YOUR CRY

I love the LORD because he hears my voice and
my prayer for mercy. Because he bends down
to listen, I will pray as long as I have breath!

—PSALM 116:1-2

DON'T KNOW IF you are paying attention to the current state of
the world right now, but it's clear we need a revival. So we cry out
for it day and night. At our church we've embraced the posture
and disposition of crying out. We cry and we cry and we cry some
more. And some may begin to wonder, "OK, are you going to stop?"
The answer is no! We will not stop until we see what we're praying
for manifest all over the earth.

This is why I love Psalm 116:1–2. It is something that I can
understand now as a father of four. I couldn't have understood it
ten years ago. When you have children, you recognize, discern, and
decipher the cries of your children, especially when they are infants
and can't talk. Infants have different cries that mean different things.
Some cries are urgent and cause us to come running. Other cries
bellow, and we know we have a couple of minutes before we're really
needed. There's a cry that says, "I'm hungry," "I'm thirsty," "I need to
be changed" (you can smell that one too), "I need to be held," "I'm
bored," or "I'm uncomfortable." The one I recognize but don't quite
understand is the "I'm sleepy" cry. Why do infants cry when they're
sleepy? Why don't they just go to sleep? That's what I do. We learn
how to interpret our children's cries, and we respond accordingly.

Our Father does the same thing with us. It amazes me. Not
only can He interpret our cries, but He remembers and answers
them. And He can distinguish our cries from everyone else's in
the world. This is also a pretty remarkable phenomenon. If you're

a parent, you can understand this on a smaller scale: your child can be with fifty other children, four of them can be crying, and you can tell which one is yours. There's something about your own child's cries that directly connects to your heart.

I'll never forget being on an airplane and hearing a child cry. The cry kind of sounded like one of my children's. I knew my child was not on the plane, but I heard a cry that sounded like my daughter's. I kept looking back, thinking, "Is my family on this flight trying to surprise me?"

> *Just as we are connected to the cries of our children, our heavenly Father is connected to ours.*

Just as we are connected to the cries of our children, it's important that we understand that our heavenly Father is connected to ours. Even as we cry out to Him during corporate worship with other believers or alone in the privacy of our prayer closets, the Lord hears us, distinguishes our cries from all others, and answers them. I want to encourage you to continue to cry out and not be silent. The Lord responds to our cries. Just as our children's cries vary in degrees of urgency, so do ours.

THE CONSISTENT CRY

In Exodus 1 the Israelites were slaves in Egypt. The Egyptians were brutal taskmasters and worked the people of Israel without mercy. For four hundred years they lived under the lash of oppression, just as the Lord had prophesied to their forefather Abraham. And they cried out to God for deliverance:

> Years passed, and the king of Egypt died. But the Israelites *continued* to groan under their burden of slavery. They cried out for help, and their cry rose up to God. God heard their groaning, and he remembered his covenant promise to Abraham, Isaac, and Jacob.
>
> —EXODUS 2:22–23, EMPHASIS ADDED

The word *continued* in this verse also points to an unyielding, consistent groan. Day after day, month after month, and year after year they cried out to God for deliverance. They never stopped crying, even though they didn't see their answer right away, even though it seemed as if God was hearing. And they continued to cry out to God until their cries met up with His set time for their deliverance. We call this a *kairos* moment.

In all of their distress they may not have been able to keep a grip on the fact that God was fulfilling His plan through them, that they were in this season as part of His sovereign design. God had made a covenant promise to their forefather, and He knew the time had come for Him to act. So God raised up a deliverer, Moses, whom He found in the middle of the desert on Mount Sinai.

We need to consistently and continually cry out until our cries meet up with God's set time. There are moments in your life when the will of God and your desires are on a collision course. And in an explosive meeting by God's design—His set time for your life or your family—breakthrough or deliverance manifests. The cry could have started with your grandparents. You may not know that, so don't stop crying. You never know when the moment will be when your cry intersects with God's set time.

As a generation, we are moving into a set time when God intends to send revival to the whole earth. Many of us can sense it, but there's also this sense that it is tarrying. *Tarry* is an old English word that means to wait or delay. So the question is, Why is revival being delayed? One of the reasons is that there is no cry. Cries are connected to an intense desire for something. And when there's no cry going up to heaven for revival, it may appear to God that perhaps we don't really want it.

Maybe there's a feeling that revival is no longer on the table. Maybe it's been such a long time coming that people have stopped crying out. But the Israelites cried out for four hundred years because they wanted what God had promised. Don't lose your cry just because it seems the answer is taking a long time.

Maybe we need to start spreading the word again that revival is available, that outpouring is available, that deliverance is available.

Maybe we need to start declaring that the year of God's favor is upon us. If people knew that these things were available, that they will surely come if we cry out, maybe they would cry out for them again.

No one likes being in bondage, so there are cries beginning to rise up from the earth. And God is beginning to respond, "I have certainly seen the oppression of my people....I am aware of their suffering. I [will] come down [and] rescue them...and lead them...into their own fertile and spacious land" (Exod. 3:7–8).

I have news for you: God hears the consistent cry. If you want to see His promise of an outpouring manifest in your lifetime, don't stop crying out!

THE PERSISTENT CRY

There is another kind of cry that is directly related to the consistent cry, and that is the persistent cry. You may know the story found in Luke 18 of the persistent widow. Usually with stories like this we don't get the moral (or the point) until the end, but Luke, the one telling us what happened, didn't care about spoilers this day. He started off with "Jesus told his disciples a story to show that they should always pray and never give up" (v. 1).

Just that much will mess with some of our theology. In certain movements it is taught that praying for something more than once shows a lack of faith. That's not true, and you may know somebody who needs to be set free from that. If this is the belief, then let's see how it plays out. Somebody comes to you and says, "Hey, I have this situation, and I really need you to agree with me in prayer." With this as your belief, you say, "It's already done." According to Scripture, because of what Jesus Christ has done, it is already done, yes. But you still have to pray about it. You have access to it, but you don't have possession of it without prayer.

So yes, Christ's work is already done, but your prayer is not. So if your friends or loved ones ask you to pray for them, don't just say, "It's already done," and keep it moving, because oftentimes that's the manifestation of "I'm not praying for you." When we're praying for someone who is going through a trial, we need to keep interceding until the person receives justice. Be persistent! This is what Jesus was saying to His disciples, and this is what He is saying to us.

Cry out until you see deliverance!

This widow kept coming to this godless, coldhearted judge, pleading for justice in a dispute she had had with an enemy. She came day after day, and day after day he ignored her. Finally he couldn't take it anymore, and he ruled justly in her favor.

> Then the Lord said, "Learn a lesson from this unjust judge. Even he rendered a just decision in the end. So don't you think God will surely give justice to his chosen people who cry out to him day and night? Will he keep putting them off? I tell you, he will grant justice to them quickly! But when the Son of Man returns, how many will he find on the earth who have faith?"
>
> —Luke 18:6–8

God is inquiring: Will He find people who will have patience and trust, knowing He's waiting for the right time to intervene and act on their behalf? Or will He find people who in their frustration stopped believing?

He is saying in this moment that we must cry out to Him day and night. If you stop crying out, you are signifying that you are frustrated with Him. You're frustrated that He's not answering on your time line. Like this widow did with the judge, cry out to God day and night. Don't stop crying out. Don't stop asking. Don't stop believing that God will answer. He's waiting on the exact right time to intervene on your behalf. He answers the persistent cry.

Stories
of the River

She was unable to make a fist—completely unable to ball her hand tightly and make a fist. She is a schoolteacher, and her students used to make fun of her for constantly dropping chalk and pens and pencils. Her story of healing is amazing. She had her eyes closed during worship when she felt someone grab her hand. Assuming it was her husband, who was standing on that side of her, she initially didn't think anything of it. However, while still feeling the sensation that someone was holding her hand, she opened her eyes and discovered that her husband had his hands lifted and his eyes closed in worship. She then realized that she was able to close her hand and make a fist, so she grabbed her husband's hand. All of this was taking place during worship. She grabbed his hand and squeezed it tightly—tightly enough to make him say, "Ow!" Then, as she squeezed his hand, he realized, "Oh my goodness, she is squeezing my hand." At the same time, she realized, "Oh my goodness, I am squeezing his hand!" I placed a picture of her closed hand on my Instagram page and wrote, "To you it's just a random fist, but to her it's something that she couldn't do for more than two years!" In one supernatural moment she was healed in the presence of the Lord. It's happening!

THE MISUNDERSTOOD CRY

Yes, there is a misunderstood cry. In 1 Samuel 1 we discover that Hannah cried out for a child in a way that the priest Eli misunderstood. The Bible says,

> As she was praying to the LORD, Eli watched her. Seeing her lips moving but hearing no sound, he thought she had

been drinking. "Must you come here drunk?" he demanded. "Throw away your wine!"

"Oh no, sir!" she replied. "I haven't been drinking wine or anything stronger. But I am very discouraged, and I was pouring out my heart to the LORD."

—1 SAMUEL 1:12–15

Are you one whose walk with God has been misunderstood? Have people misunderstood why you live the way you live? People don't understand why you do the things you do. They don't understand why you keep crying out to God the way you do. People can't figure you out. They don't understand why you're not happy with things the way they are. Why are you always asking for more?

This is how Hannah's husband responded to her:

"Why are you crying, Hannah?" Elkanah would ask. "Why aren't you eating? Why be downhearted just because you have no children? You have me—isn't that better than having ten sons?"

—1 SAMUEL 1:8

The only one who understood her cry was God. No one but God understood what she longed for. Her cry was for something that man could not give.

If this story resonates with you, then trust that you are not alone. As it was with Hannah, there's something on the inside of you that longs for more. You were created to birth something in the earth. This season of barrenness has caused you to not want to eat or be around other people. What God is stirring in you is something that cannot be fulfilled by man.

The misunderstood cry is really the unselfish cry.

Another thing about the misunderstood cry is that it's not even for you. The whole reason Hannah was crying was not even to benefit herself. Her cry was ultimately an unselfish cry. Her desire was to be part of what God was doing in the earth during that time. She wanted to birth someone who would faithfully serve the

Lord—and she wanted to give what God birthed through her right back to Him. That's exactly what she did. God gave her a son, whom she named Samuel, and he became one of the greatest prophets in Israel's history.

God understands your cry.

You may be crying out in the house of the Lord, going to the altar even when there's no invitation or altar call. People don't understand why you're crying and praying. They don't understand that there's something on the inside of you that longs for more. I believe that God gave me a revelation about this cry especially for you whose cries are misunderstood. He wants you to know that He understands your cries and He will answer. You long to birth something in the earth that gives glory to God.

You were created to birth something in the earth.

Even though you're misunderstood, keep crying. Even though people talk about you, keep crying. Even though people don't understand your posture before the Lord, keep crying out to God. Don't let any accusations of being religiously zealous stop you from crying out to God. They may not understand now, but the thing you're going to birth will shake the nations. Keep crying.

THE DESPERATE CRY

Desperation has a sound attached to it and is not quiet. In fact, you could say that desperation is a misunderstood cry as well. The story of Bartimaeus in Mark 10:46–52, which is very dear to me and to our church, helps us understand the desperate cry. I wrote and recorded a song called "I Don't Mind Waiting" on my *Sounds of Revival* CD, and in it I exhorted from this particular passage about the desperate cry. This is a cry that recognizes that when Jesus is coming near, that is not the time to be quiet because no one else can do for you what He can. And so when those who are desperate sense His presence is near, you will have to excuse them because they will likely get loud. Their faith is coming alive!

If we can imagine the scene from Bartimaeus's perspective, it makes perfect sense. He had been hearing about what Jesus could do. He'd been hearing about what happened to people when they got in His presence. Though he was blind and could only hear and feel the growing anticipation of the crowd, he was not going to let that moment or a season of manifestation pass Him by. The closer Jesus got, the louder the crowd got. Somehow he had to get the Lord's attention because He was the only One who could give him sight. His desperation grew by the minute, and just when the moment reached its set time, he cried out, "Son of David, have mercy upon me!"

Many told him to be quiet, but the closer Jesus came, the louder Bartimaeus cried out. Oftentimes desperate people expose non-desperate people. The ones telling him to be quiet couldn't do anything for him. They knew him as a beggar. They could give him pocket change but not real change. Only Jesus could do that, which is why Bartimaeus had to ignore them. When you're desperate for an encounter with God, there will be times when you will have to ignore those around you. When you recognize that Jesus is the only One who can change you, the opinion of others ceases to matter. Sometimes the very reason you're being told to tone down your worship, prayer, and desperation is because it causes others to become uncomfortable with their lack of desperation. I don't know about you, but I refuse to remain quiet in this moment when I'm aware that Jesus is passing by. I refuse to miss this moment. Bartimaeus got Jesus's attention. I want the same thing to happen when I cry out.

Jesus heard him and asked, "What do you want Me to do for you?

Bartimaeus did not stutter: "I want to see!"

Jesus said, "Go, for your faith has healed you."

Bartimaeus was crying out because he was desperate. But Bartimaeus was also crying out because he had faith. He had been desperate the entire time. He had been desperate his entire life. And when he heard that Jesus was near, desperation got a voice.

Perhaps you've been known to be reserved, but as Jesus comes closer and the visitation of God comes, that's not the time to keep your reputation of being reserved. You may have never shouted in your life, but that won't matter. All that will matter is that Jesus is near and you need to get His attention. Let desperation for the presence of God arise in you until it finds a voice. I am sure Bartimaeus's cry was so loud that it made the people around him uncomfortable. But he wasn't about to miss a once-in-a-lifetime opportunity with the only person who could give him what he needed. He was not going to let pride, embarrassment, a reputation of composure, or anything else get in the way of his miracle.

THE CRY OF FAITH

The secret power of the cry of faith is that it allows you to reach into the future and pull into your present the grace and provision God has promised to release at a later time. God does not live within the constraints of time as we do. He is omnipresent. He's everywhere at the same time. And because there is no sequential order in eternity, everything in Him is accessible consistently, all the time, at the same time, and outside of time. Time is a servant to faith. The Gentile woman in Matthew 15:21–28 had a supernatural awareness of this principle, and she used it to claim deliverance for her demonized daughter.

When Jesus is near, desperation gets a voice.

When the woman first approached Jesus, asking Him to heal her demon-possessed daughter, He ignored her. It seems strange to us that Jesus seemed to be giving someone who came to Him in faith and sincerity the cold shoulder. It seems so out of character for Him. There are theories on what message He was sending in that moment. But that's not our focus.

The woman came to Him in faith, recognizing that He was the Son of David. We also see in verse 27 that she acknowledged to whom He was sent—and it wasn't her and her people. But her response is one of faith that communicates a future truth. When she said, "Even dogs are allowed to eat the scraps that fall beneath their masters' table," she was speaking of a time yet to come when the Gentiles would have access to the promises of God through faith. She was declaring to Him that despite her present unworthiness, she needed to make a demand on a future provision and make it apply to her present need.

She couldn't wait because her daughter was severely possessed right then, and her faith told her that Jesus had the capacity to answer her cry right then. Even though her initial question was met with silence, she did not let that keep her from crying out, believing He was the Son of God. She believed that what was promised in the future could be made manifest to her right then.

Sometimes we get into the presence of God, knowing we don't deserve what we are asking for. But as we get in a posture of worship, acknowledging God for who He is, our worship begins to build our faith. And by faith we are able to cry out, and what may not be fully manifested to us right now we reach into the future and pull into our present because it is consistently available in God.

You may feel as if God has been silent when you have cried out to Him, but keep crying in faith. Even when you don't get an answer right away, throw yourself down before God and say, "I know who You are, I know to whom You've been sent, I know I have access, and I know You can do this for me."

THE PROPHETIC CRY

Some have a cry that I call the prophetic cry. It can be a combination of the misunderstood and desperate cries, and it comes because what you've seen and heard in the spirit has not yet manifested as a reality on the earth. You've seen something, and you've heard something in the spirit during your personal times of encountering God in worship and prayer. But things here don't yet look like what you've seen or experienced. This is what happened to the prophet Isaiah.

In Isaiah 6 the prophet describes a heavenly encounter.

In the year that King Uzziah died I saw the Lord sitting on
a throne, high and lifted up, and His train filled the temple.
Above it stood the seraphim. Each one had six wings. With
two he covered his face, and with two he covered his feet,
and with two he flew. One cried to another and said: "Holy,
holy, holy, is the Lord of Hosts; the whole earth is full
of His glory." The posts of the door moved at the voice of
him who cried, and the house was filled with smoke. And I
said: "Woe is me! For I am undone because I am a man of
unclean lips, and I dwell in the midst of a people of unclean
lips. For my eyes have seen the King, the Lord of Hosts."
Then one of the seraphim flew to me with a live coal which
he had taken with the tongs from off the altar in his hand.
And he laid it on my mouth, and said, "This has touched
your lips, and your iniquity is taken away, and your sin
purged." Also I heard the voice of the Lord saying, "Whom
shall I send, and who will go for us?" Then I said, "Here
am I. Send me."

—Isaiah 6:1–8, mev

Isaiah had a vision of an open heaven and received a glimpse of
the eternal, a glimpse of the divine, a glimpse of the majesty of God.
He was given a glimpse of the beauty of holiness.

By design an open heaven can be an invitation by God meant to
awaken awe, awaken wonder, awaken desire, and speak to the deep
longing of our hearts. For Isaiah it was an invitation to embrace his
prophetic assignment.

One can only imagine what life was like for Isaiah after his
encounter. When you have a genuine encounter with God, not only
does it change you, but you can never forget it. It will shape how you
think, act, and live. Isaiah had a personal encounter with God that
changed the trajectory of his life.

In Isaiah 64 he writes these words:

Oh, that you would burst from the heavens and come
down! How the mountains would quake in your presence!
As fire causes wood to burn and water to boil, your coming

would make the nations tremble. Then your enemies would learn the reason for your fame!

—Isaiah 64:1–2

Oh, that you would rip open the heavens and descend, make the mountains shudder at your presence—as when a forest catches fire, as when fire makes a pot to boil—to shock your enemies into facing you, make the nations shake in their boots!

—Isaiah 64:1–2, The Message

Oh, that You would rend the heavens! That You would come down! That the mountains might shake at Your presence—as fire burns brushwood, as fire causes water to boil—to make Your name known to Your adversaries, that the nations may tremble at Your presence!

—Isaiah 64:1–2, nkjv

We are reading the words of a person who is still consumed by what he saw the year King Uzziah died. He is still consumed by his encounter when he says, "Oh, that You would burst from the heavens and come down. Rend the heavens. Rip open the heavens!" This is a cry that says, "I've seen something that makes my insides feel like they are going to burst! I've seen something that causes me to yearn for more! To cry out for more! To search for more!" He's saying, "I long for the day when You will give us more than a glimpse of heaven. I long for the day when You will give us more than a glimpse of eternity. I long for the day when everyone will see what I've seen!"

Isaiah saw something during his personal encounter that wasn't yet happening around him, so he cried out for it. In Isaiah chapter 6 he said, "I saw the Lord." Yet there was something in him that said, "I long for the day when *all* will see the Lord."

You could sense Isaiah's passion as he was saying, "I pray and cry out because of what I saw *and* what I heard! I saw the Lord seated high, and I saw the cherubim. But it's what I heard them say that stirs me as much as what I saw! I saw the Lord. He was sitting on a lofty throne, and the train of His robe filled the temple. Attending Him were mighty seraphim, each having six wings. With two wings they covered their faces, with two they covered their feet, and with two they flew. They were calling out to each other, 'Holy, holy, holy is the LORD of heaven's armies! The whole earth is filled with His glory!' They said, 'Holy is the Lord. The whole *earth* is full of His glory.' If they had said, 'The highest heaven is full of His glory,' my singular cry would be to go there. But the fact that the earth is full of the glory says the glory is coming, so I cry, 'Oh, that You would rend the heavens, burst out, rip open the heavens!'"

Isaiah had a cry: "Oh, that others could see what I've seen, feel what I've felt, experience what I've experienced." Those who have had genuine encounters with God are crying out that everyone would have the kind of transforming encounters they've had. It seems the feeling is if others would have the same encounter, they wouldn't think our passion was weird or strange. They likely wouldn't think this pursuit of God was too much. They would understand this passion. Isaiah was saying, "Oh, God, let others in on it! I can't keep it to myself." He had a prophetic cry.

THE CRY OF CREATION AND THE SPIRIT

There is another cry—one beyond our understanding. It is a deep, wordless cry, a cry that is not even coming from us. In Romans 8:19–26 the Bible says:

> For all creation is waiting eagerly for that future day when God will reveal who his children really are. Against its will, all creation was subjected to God's curse. But with eager hope, the creation looks forward to the day when it will join God's children in glorious freedom from death and decay. For we know that all creation has been groaning as in the pains of childbirth right up to the present time. And we believers also groan.... But the Holy Spirit prays for us with groanings that cannot be expressed in words.

Groanings are deep, wailing cries, "a crying out in grief."[1] Creation is crying, we are crying, and the Spirit is crying for the same thing—for the manifestation of the sons of God.

We cry out because we know the way things are is not the way they are supposed to be.

The reason we cry out is because we know the way things are right now is not the way they are supposed to be. That we all are crying out signifies that we're in harmony with what God is doing.

The earth and the Spirit have been crying out on our behalf, and even though there have been some outbreaks of crying out among God's people, we need more. God is restoring these six cries to His people. These are the cries that get Him to hear, stop, and ask, "What do you want Me to do for you?" These cries are how we get in harmony with what God is doing. Creation is crying. The Spirit is crying. Now, I believe, the people of God will cry out more than ever, and we will see an outpouring of the Holy Spirit in our generation.

RESPOND

If you've been crying out to God, wondering when you will see miracles, deliverance, and the promise of God birthed, you join with creation and the Spirit, who've been eagerly waiting for us to arise and take up our full rights as God's children. As your Father, God hears every one of your cries and is coming to answer you. Don't be afraid to lift your voice and cry out. Whether your cry is misunderstood, consistent, persistent, or desperate, find your place, and cry out to God. Creation, the Spirit, and the people of God form a three-note chord when they cry out in harmony. Are you willing to join the cry with creation and the Spirit?

Revival has been waiting, but we have the key to unlock the door of revival. It's when we join in the harmony of the Spirit and creation and cry out to God for more. In the body of Christ we've only scratched the surface. We've only had one glance of the Savior's eyes. We may have tasted of God's glory, but let's cry out for more!

CHAPTER 4

FOLLOW THE PATHWAY

*Search me, O God, and know my heart; test
me and know my anxious thoughts. Point out
anything in me that offends you, and lead
me along the path of everlasting life.*

—PSALM 139:23–24

WHEN THE LORD sovereignly decided to dwell with us at Deeper, I began to revisit the stories of the revivalists God has used throughout the last four hundred years. One in particular stood out. His name was John G. Lake. God used him to spread the gospel in Africa. In a span of five years he planted 625 churches and raised up 1,250 preachers. After the five years in Africa, Lake moved to Spokane, Washington. Praying for people, he established something called healing rooms, and God used him to see one hundred thousand healing miracles in five years. At the time, newspapers reported that Spokane was the healthiest city in the world because no one was sick.[1]

As of the writing of this book, our church has seen more than two hundred miracles in less than two years. But John G. Lake saw one hundred thousand miracles in five years. It is apparent to me that we are only seeing a glimpse. We have only scratched the surface. The question God has been asking us is, "Are you *still* hungry?" Two hundred miracles is only enough to build faith for more. We know that God never intended to do great things only for our eight hundred to one thousand members. As those whom God has chosen to visit, we accept the responsibility to do whatever it takes to unlock the pathway to more. We have no interest in the move of God stopping with us.

We learned in those early months of revival that God was giving us an invitation to a perpetual outpouring, and now He is extending it to all who are being moved and impassioned by our testimonies. But the invitation is connected to something we don't like to talk about much anymore. The invitation to seeing a perpetual outpouring of God in this generation is connected to repentance. Outpouring happens only for those who are willing to give themselves completely to God, and this happens through the vehicle of repentance. If we are unwilling to let go of the things that obscure our view of God or we find ourselves in a place where we can enter His presence and remain obstinate about the things He is requiring of us, then revival will have an expiration date. It will die. But we have a choice whether to let revival live or die.

LEGACY OR HEADSTONE?

In the history of the world's revivals some revivals sparked lasting movements, and others died. Some revivals have legacies; other revivals have headstones. The revivals that have headstones are the ones that have a definitive start and a definitive end but leave no lasting legacy. Revival can leave a legacy. Some awakenings become perpetual and create a culture and don't just mark a moment in time.

If you were to ask people if they want revival, the overwhelming answer would likely be yes. However, there is a pathway to revival, and that is repentance. Repentance is the pathway to righteousness, mercy, salvation, and restoration, and it is the pathway to revival. You can't have any of these things without repentance. We don't like to talk about repentance because it doesn't make us feel good, but God is not interested in how we feel. He's interested in truth in the inward parts (Ps. 51:6).

When God decides sovereignly to show up in a particular place and reveal Himself, we have an opportunity to decide how we will respond to the revelation. In Isaiah 6:1–5 we are shown how the prophet Isaiah responded when God chose to transport him into His presence. Verse 1 says, "It was in the year King Uzziah died that I *saw* the Lord" (emphasis added). Notice it doesn't say "sought." Isaiah's encounter didn't happen because of what Isaiah was doing. God showed up because God wanted Isaiah to see and experience Him. Isaiah saw the majesty of God because God decided it was time.

This passage in Isaiah 6 reveals the moment Isaiah was called to prophesy to his nation. To equip Isaiah for this, God allowed him to see something bigger. He allowed him to see something that changed him. He allowed him to experience something that would mark his life forever. Isaiah saw what very few see, and as a result of being in the presence of God, Isaiah came to a finite conclusion. He said, "It's all over! I am doomed, for I am a sinful man. I have filthy lips" (v. 5). He became aware that in light of God's holiness he was not holy.

> *Outpouring happens only for those who are willing to give themselves completely to God, and this happens through the vehicle of repentance.*

There's something about being in God's presence that unlocks an awareness of our gross separation from the holiness of God. Outside of God's presence we may feel confident that we know about God and His ways. Some of us have been trained in Christian traditions from young ages. But all of that flies out the window when our humanity comes in contact with God's divinity. We cannot contain all that God is, and our humanity dies. Exodus 33:20 says that no one can see God and live. Isaiah was well aware of this. So his statement was legitimate: "I am doomed" (Isa. 6:5). It was as if he were asking, "Did You bring me here to kill me?" He knew who he was in relation to who God is. And his sense of his depraved humanity grew the longer he stayed there. Not only did he become aware that he had filthy lips, but he also became aware that he lived among a people with filthy lips. But what happened to Isaiah next is huge:

> Then one of the seraphim flew to me with a burning coal he had taken from the altar with a pair of tongs. He touched my lips with it and said, "See, this coal has touched your lips. Now your guilt is removed, and your sins are forgiven."
> —ISAIAH 6:6–7

The angel took the coal with the tongs and touched Isaiah's lips as if to say, "Be quiet, or you will miss why you have been invited into this place." Then the angel sensed Isaiah's repentant heart and took the exchange further, removing guilt and forgiving his sins. There always is a test when humanity comes in contact with divinity. The test is, Will we worship, or will we be prideful? Isaiah was completely undone. He could not move on. He had never encountered something so much higher, deeper, holier—so infinitely "more" than he was in every way. He had been humbled to the point where he was emptied of himself enough to hear the Lord asking, "Whom should I send as a messenger to this people? Who will go for us?" Isaiah swiftly replied, "Here I am. Send me" (Isa. 6:8).

If Isaiah got caught up in where he was and what he may have done to get there, he would have missed the very thing for which God had called him. Many of us get stopped at the place where we saw something, and we run out before we hear what God wants to say. But God invited Isaiah there and tested him. Isaiah's response was in proportion to how human he felt next to God's holy divinity. He took the same posture as the psalmist, who said, "Search me, O God, and know my heart....Point out anything in me that offends you" (Ps. 139:23–24). Isaiah knew he was in a delicate moment that could instantly be taken away if he did not take the right posture, which was repentance. It is clear from Isaiah's response—"Here I am. Send me."—that he didn't want anything in him to block what God wanted to do.

A Call to Greater

God showed up for Isaiah to call him to greater. God showed up at Deeper to call us to greater. God is showing up for you right where you are, calling you to greater. The first thing God gives is a glimpse of His glory. The next thing He gives is a test of humility, and finally He gives the assignment.

The first twelve months of God's outpouring on our church was only a glimpse of His glory, despite all that the Lord has done. And where we stand right now on the pathway to revival is a test of humility: Will we think that what we've seen God do so far is because of us? Will we somehow believe it is due to something we've done? Or will we humble ourselves and let go of our false sense of worthiness to be carriers of revival?

> *If God is doing it anywhere, He can do it here in my home, my church, and my community.*

In ourselves we are not worthy carriers of the river of God, but because of the new covenant, Jesus makes us righteous. I don't want you to be beaten down, but I do need you to understand that righteousness is obtained by faith in Christ. We demonstrate this faith by repenting and receiving His forgiveness, thereby becoming worthy to carry revival. On our own, though, and without repentance we are unworthy.

God is inviting us to decide if we want to see the glimpse of glory transform into a perpetual legacy of revival. Or should He just put a headstone at the place we think our formula brought His presence? Hear me by the Spirit of God: when the Lord asks if we are still hungry, He should not get a flippant response. He is asking us this question so we can say, "Search me, O God. Is there anything in me that is blocking the reality of what You want to do?" Why? Because what God wants to do among us is so much greater than what we've seen. We've seen just a glimpse.

- -

Stories
of the River

The outpouring had begun in May of 2016, and we were experiencing an incredible outpouring of the Spirit of God. In September of that year we were having our annual Habitation Conference, and my close friend David Diga Hernandez was one of our guests. He has a gift of healing, among other gifts God has given him, and during the conference he noticed one of our volunteers, Ms. Pam, who earlier had suffered a stroke, moving through the church with her cane. He called for her to come up to the platform, and he prayed for her, and instantly her partial paralysis was healed before our eyes.

We all watched Ms. Pam do things we had never seen her do. She walked without her cane, lifted her leg, and walked sideways—all things she could not do previously because of her stroke. Today Ms. Pam is down front during worship, jumping, leaping, and praising God. She's free from the confining limitations of paralysis due to a stroke. She no longer has to use the handicapped parking when she goes places. She is now one of the people who transcribes every prophetic word given in our church. Every single Sunday she is a physical reminder that it's happening!

RIGHTEOUS ENVY—COVETING THE MOVE OF GOD

For many of us what I am talking about may seem like such a far-off thing, but that's why I started the chapter with the story of John G. Lake. There must be something inside of you that stirs up righteous envy.

I was sharing with my good friends David and Nicole Binion on a pretty regular basis the many miracles that were taking place weekly at our church. Then one day David said, "My friend, I have righteous envy hearing about the things God is doing!" I thought, "Wow, *righteous envy*. What a term." It almost seems like an oxymoron, when you think about it. In Scripture envy is usually presented as a sinful behavior—wanting what someone else has. However, I discovered that God will do something for someone else, or in someone or someplace else, and seeing what He does will cause you to desire Him to do the same thing for you. Sometimes you don't know you want something until you see it.

There needs to be something that rises up in you and causes you to declare, "If God is doing it anywhere, He can do it here in my home, my church, and my community." God will sometimes use others to do extraordinary things to cause you to long for those kinds of miracles yourself. He'll put you in circles and rooms with people who operate in ways you know you are called to operate in, ways that you know God has shown you.

Repentance is an invitation to stay.

He does this to make you jealous for it. God, infinite in His wisdom, will actually bless someone to make you want the blessing. Sometimes God blesses somebody with the blessing He promised you to show you that you need to get into alignment. There is a pattern for this: Romans 11 tells us that the Gentiles—those who are not Jewish by birth—have been grafted in to make the Jewish people jealous. He wants them to see the relationship they could have with Him so He can gather them back. Righteous envy can be frustrating, but what will you do with your frustration? Will you be mad at God, or will you repent?

God is doing things in the earth to make you jealous—things that will stir your desire for Him to move in your life in such a way that when you see somebody sick, you have enough boldness to pray for them. We are seeing a powerless generation because we are running away from the very gift God has given us—the gift called repentance. Repentance is an invitation to stay. Repentance is a hard teaching for those of us in this generation. We don't like to feel bad about anything. If anything makes us feel bad, then we want to stop engaging in that activity and start doing something that gives us pleasure. But the Scripture says it's in the presence of the Lord that we find a fullness of joy and at His right hand are pleasures forevermore (Ps. 16:11). This means if you go outside of God to find pleasure, that's probably where you need to repent.

GOD IS NEAR

If repentance is an invitation, then conviction is the sign that God is near. If you enter the presence of God, begin to worship, and get a spiritual picture of sin, this is not simply guilt you feel. It is an indication that God is near you. We have to retrain ourselves. We keep thinking, "O God, I can't come close to You because I feel guilty." No. If you can lean in and see the scriptural principle, you will realize that the reason you feel guilty is because God is near you. Your humanity has come in contact with His divinity. Conviction is the appropriate response.

Conviction is the sign that God is near.

If a person can enter the presence of God and not feel anything about the porn he just watched, he ought to be afraid. His conscience has been seared. The Bible calls that a reprobate mind (Rom. 1:28). The conviction of the Holy Spirit that causes us to feel guilty is an invitation to stay in His presence *if we repent!* Guilt means He is shining a light on areas that are incongruent. He is shining a light on the very thing that will put a headstone on revival for you.

Repentance is a gift from God. It is an invitation from God for salvation, righteousness, mercy, restoration, and revival. God is not interested in a generation showing up to attend a revival; God wants revival to be in you. Revival is not a show put on by a few anointed people. Revival is something that happens in your spirit man. You who were once dead are now made alive. You whose affections have grown cold are now hot for Christ. You who were cold are now on fire. Revival is something that happens on the inside of you, and it is contagious! You cannot be near fire and not feel it.

WORSHIP DOES NOT REPLACE REPENTANCE

God says to this generation that our deeds don't vindicate us. What you do doesn't make you right. Your worship doesn't replace repentance. We are the generation that has more written material on worship than any other in history, yet we are the generation that, based on its fruit, seems to be resisting God the most. In Psalm 50:8–10 God says:

I have no complaint about your sacrifices or the burnt
offerings you constantly offer. But I do not need the bulls
from your barns or the goats from your pens. For all the
animals of the forest are mine, and I own the cattle on a
thousand hills.

It's not our worship that God has a problem with. He doesn't
have a complaint about our external things. And really, He doesn't
need them. We don't serve a narcissistic God who needs us to lift
our hands for Him to feel good today, as if He's the king and we're
court jesters. "Sing for Me. Shout for Me. I need to feel better today."
No! God is God, and we are not. We have needs; He does not.
What God is saying in Psalm 50 is that our worship has become rit-
ualistic. We are doing things externally that are disconnected from
the internal posture of our hearts.

God really does not care how high we lift our hands or how loud
we sing, if we don't mean it. God is not interested in ritual; He's
interested in relationship. This is why David has such an amazing
revelation in Psalm 51:16–17: "You do not desire a sacrifice, or I
would offer one. You do not want a burnt offering. The sacrifice you
desire is a broken spirit. You will not reject a broken and repentant
heart, O God."

What God is looking for are people who recognize that they need
Him. David came to an amazing revelation because at that time,
according to the Law, God did require a blood sacrifice. But David
saw more. He saw that God desired something from the inside.

God is not looking for people who are going through the motions—
the motions of revival, the motions of outpouring—doing what they
think He wants to see, saying what they think He wants to hear.
God is looking for those who will say, "God, search me. If there's
anything in me that offends You, take it away from me."

If we come into God's presence and do the acts of worship without
repentance, it's ritual because our hearts are not right. We are not
intimately and honestly engaged—in spirit and truth—with God.
We can lift our hands all day, but worship does not replace repentance. As one Bible dictionary says, "In its biblical sense repentance

refers to a deeply seated and thorough turning from self to God."[2] Repentance leads you to say, "God, whatever You desire from me or whatever You're shining a light on, I will not hold on to it more than I hold on to You." In repentance you are saying, "Search me," and God tells you what should remain. Our response should be that we turn away from whatever He tells us to release in order to hold on to Him.

The result of repentance is salvation—salvation from being ensnared by the idols you've been worshipping, the things that have been blocking your view of God, and the things in your heart that have been keeping you from being used by God. This is why God gives you a glimpse of His glory. He makes it so amazing that we long for it, so much so that we will do whatever it takes to stay in that moment—including repent. God allows us to be stirred up with righteous envy so we'll say: "I want to see revival come in my life and lifetime. God, if You're doing it somewhere, do it in me. If there's anything in me that offends You, take it out of me so You will bring revival in me."

The apostle John wrote:

> If we claim we have no sin, we are only fooling ourselves and not living in the truth. But if we confess our sins to him, he is faithful and just to forgive us our sins and to cleanse us from all wickedness. If we claim we have not sinned, we are calling God a liar and showing that his word has no place in our hearts.
>
> —1 John 1:8–10

Exposed!

I have seen something, and it overwhelms me. It makes me want to cry. It makes me want to cry out. It makes me want to lie on my face. But mainly it makes me want to stop doing anything and everything that would possibly get in the way of it. There are moments in our lives when God shines light on something and says, "I want that." It may be a habit or way of thinking—it could be anything that is separating you from Him. There are times and seasons when God in His mercy will expose things that are hindering our relationship with Him, and we hate exposure. We want to deal with everything in private, but if God can't get your attention in private or you won't honor Him enough in private, He may expose you in public so you will return to Him.

It is human nature to hide from God, but we can't do what seems natural. We also try to hide from one another. That is why in the Garden of Eden, Adam and Eve sewed fig leaves together to hide from each other. We don't want our sin to be exposed to others. We can't hide anything from God, so we try to hide our sin from one another. That's why God connects righteousness and effective prayer when He says, "Confess your faults one to another" (James 5:16, KJV). An unrepentant heart can keep you from seeing the answers to your prayers concerning revival.

The Lord is showing us that He wants to do something great among us, but the pathway to it is the very thing that most of us run from. You would probably shout if I said the pathway to revival is praise or more worship. If the pathway was more prayer, others might say, "OK, I can do that." But the moment we discover the pathway to revival is repentance, most of us say, "Oh." But if you are hungry for revival, you are ready to do whatever God desires of you to see His glory come.

RESPOND

What is standing in the way of revival for you? Don't allow any unconfessed sin to cause God to look at your worship as a ritual. I believe there are things the Lord has been showing you for quite some time that you have been resisting. What if I told you that the next outpouring is connected to your surrender? What if I told you that the level of outpouring you experience is directly connected to the level of surrender and truth you are willing to walk in with God?

God wants to use you. The Bible says the same spirit that raised Christ from the dead lives in you (Rom. 8:11), not only in the pastor, bishop, apostle, or prophet. You are part of the chain of humanity through which God will bring the next habitation of His Spirit.

This is the season of the corporate anointing. The next move of God will not be predicated on the individual. In many of our churches the ministry offices have been exalted almost to the level of being worshipped, causing people to believe that God could not use someone who was not operating in one of the fivefold ministry gifts the same way He uses apostles, prophets, evangelists, pastors, and teachers. But God is taking the needle and thread from those who are trying to re-stitch the veil that was torn when Christ died. (See Matthew 27:51.) They are doing this to make themselves more important, but there is only one High Priest, and it's not a man. Jesus Christ is the High Priest. He is our Mediator, our Intercessor. He is the One who makes the way for all of us to enter heaven's most holy place.

The level of outpouring you experience is directly connected to the level of surrender and truth you are willing to walk in with God.

The greatest revival that is going to happen in the earth is going to happen through God's surrendered corporate church. God wants to do greater. This means this word about repentance is not for the few. It's for all. What glimpses God has shown us are to make you long for more. He let us witness ten, twenty, fifty, or one hundred miracles so we could long for one hundred thousand. If you're hungry for it, be honest and say, "I want that, Lord. Do it in me. Do it in us."

This is the prayer God is requiring of us:

> Search me, O God, and know my heart; test me and know my anxious thoughts. Point out anything in me that offends you, and lead me along the path of everlasting life.
> —PSALM 139:23–24

God is looking for people who will say, "Whatever You want, God, You can have." Your decision determines whether the current move of God will be perpetual or if a headstone will be put in place. I invite you to the spiritual altar, out of your comfort zone and your hiding place. I invite you to offer up to God anything that separates you from experiencing His greater outpouring. God wants to bring a great revival through you. Do you want what God has for you more than what you have right now? If so, I invite you to repent.

CHAPTER 5

IT'S ALL ABOUT CAPACITY—
HOW EMPTY ARE YOU?

And Elisha said, "Borrow as many empty jars as
you can from your friends and neighbors. Then go
into your house with your sons and shut the door
behind you. Pour olive oil from your flask into the
jars, setting each one aside when it is filled." So she
did as she was told....Soon every container was full
to the brim!...And then the olive oil stopped flowing.

—2 KINGS 4:3-6

THE BIBLE SAYS God doesn't do anything without engaging
His servants in His plans (Amos 3:7). Though God is God
all by Himself, He desires to partner with us. Much of His
movement in the earth happens as we submit ourselves as vessels
through which He can flow. The Bible is a chronicle of the works of
God extended through man. And history shows that revival spreads
by the preaching and teaching of men and women who've been lit on
fire by the Spirit of God.

If you have cried out for revival and been in the room as intercession and worship were being offered up, you probably have felt a
longing in your heart to be used by God. It is during these moments
that you may cry out, "I want more of You, God," or, "I want to be
used by You, Lord." But do we? Do we know what it will take to
make room for the fullness of God in our lives?

We are entering a season when we cannot instinctually answer
the question "Do you want to be used by God?" Our participation
in this next move of God cannot be by default. Our alignment with
what God is doing must be intentional and deliberate. God blesses
with more of Him those who recognize their need for Him. Those

who are empty, those who are spiritually bankrupt, those who can say, "I need God more than anything else"—these are the people God wants to fill and use for His glory.

I remember growing up with an insatiable desire to be in the presence of God. My mom did not have to drag me to church. I used to play church all the time. I remember setting up my green army men not for war but as a choir, and I would stand in front of them, directing them. When I did go to church, I always tried to be close to someone I knew was being used by God. I just wanted to be near the person's gifting and anointing. There is something contagious about the anointing, and I hoped to have whatever that person had.

But being used by God is not about how we feel; it's about our capacity. My son loves pizza; he is a pizza-eating machine. When he was six, he ate as if he were sixteen. People ask me what I am going to do, how I am going to keep him fed. I tell them, "I'm going to keep writing songs." One day he ate slice after slice and kept asking for more. My wife and I were surprised he could eat that much. At one point I told him to slow down, but he kept asking for more. Finally he had his fill, but he must not have realized he had surpassed what his stomach could hold, and he threw up everywhere. He didn't have the capacity to hold what he wanted. He had the desire for more pizza but not the capacity to receive it.

Many of us are in the same boat. We're saying, "God, fill me. Use me. I want more of You." But do we have the capacity to handle more of God? Let me show you something in Scripture.

ONLY EMPTY VESSELS CAN BE FILLED

Second Kings 4:1–7 tells the story of a woman who was recently widowed. She had two sons and was in debt. According to Jewish law, if a person had a debt but no money to pay it, he would have to work it off as an indentured or indebted servant. But here in 2 Kings 4 the creditors were threatening to take it a step further and make this woman and her sons slaves. In the moment of her desperation the woman cried out to God, who in those days was represented by the prophets, the men of God. She said, in essence, "I need God to intervene. My husband was righteous, but I'm in this desperate situation. I'm not trying to figure it out for myself. We are hungry, and we have nothing left." The woman's desperation and awareness of the little she had gave her enormous capacity to receive what she needed from God. She was aware of her need for God to work a miracle in her life.

Those of us who are becoming aware of our need for God must learn to live in a consistent posture of crying out and expectation. Expectation is an anticipation of being filled by God every day, like a chick that waits in the nest for the mother bird to return with food. We pray, "Give us this day our daily bread" (Matt. 6:11, KJV). This is not a one-time cry. We need God daily. Do you live with that daily expectation? Are you, moment by moment, crying out, "God, I need You"?

The woman in 2 Kings 4 found herself in this place of emptiness. All she had was a flask of oil, and the prophet said, "I can work with that." This oil is a spiritual representation of the anointing of God that imbues us with the power of God so we can do mighty exploits in His name. So yes, God can work with the little we have. It's a start, but then we see in verse 3 that the man of God, the prophet Elisha, told the woman, "Borrow as many empty jars as you can from your friends and neighbors." A little oil is better than no oil, but a little is not enough. Like the woman, we need to increase our capacity.

Only empty vessels can receive what God wants to give.

How many times have we come before God saying we want to be used by Him, but we are full of the cares of life—full of worry, pride, greed, envy, jealousy, and all the works of the flesh? God wants to give us more of Himself—His anointing, power, miracles, provision, healing, blessing—but sometimes we are already filled to the top with so many other things. You can't be filled with the oil of God while still being full of yourself.

Stories
of the River

Each month at our church we host what we call Presence Nights. People gather from around Central Florida and even from other states and countries for these services. Presence Nights are always marked by anticipation and expectation. People line up outside for hours prior to the service just to get in. There is no agenda at these services but to seek God, hear from God, and respond accordingly. And God always does something amazing on Presence Nights, even though we never fully know what to expect.

On one particular night, my friend Caleb had a word of knowledge that the Lord wanted to heal paralysis. We've seen people come in using wheelchairs, walkers, and canes and walk out healed. Interestingly that particular night we didn't visibly see anyone who seemed paralyzed, but we knew God had spoken, so in faith we prayed that God would reverse paralysis.

After the prayer we asked for anyone in the room who had that condition to identify himself. In the back of the room a man raised his hand and then came forward. He was a musician. He played the keyboard, and something happened that caused his hand to become locked and paralyzed, but the Lord healed him that night. We all watched him open and shut his hand and move his fingers—all things he could not do before that.

Several months later Caleb and I went out to eat at Red Robin and ran into this gentleman who was healed. We didn't actually recognize him because he had only been visiting our church. He came up to us and said, "You are the guy that prayed for me, and I was healed!" He introduced us to those who were with him and shared the testimony again. He was still healed. It's happening!

GET USED TO FEELING EMPTY

Some of us hate the feeling of emptiness. It carries a negative connotation in our culture, but emptiness is the prerequisite to receiving more from God. Emptiness gives you capacity. The emptier you are, the more room you have to be filled. Matthew 5:6 says, "Blessed are those who hunger and thirst for righteousness [the ways of God], for they will be filled" (NIV).

Emptiness is the requirement for receiving the oil of God.

If you want to be used by God, you must become acquainted with feeling empty. You will not recognize your need for God until you are empty. As Matthew 5:6 implies, feeling empty is the same as feeling hungry or thirsty. You need food and water. You need to be nourished. You need to be filled. When you are thirsty and you drink soda instead of water, for the moment, your body does not feel as if it needs water, even though it does. The soda temporarily quenched your thirst, but it also cheated your body out of what it really needed to be filled, nourished, and satisfied. In this same way you won't really recognize your spiritual needs if you are filled with other things.

Some of us are trying to medicate our way out of feeling empty. We may try to drink our way out of it. We try to fill ourselves with everything else, including the lust of the flesh and the pride of life, and then we wonder why there's no authority, power, miracles, and presence manifesting in our lives. Filling ourselves with anything other than God says we don't want His oil and we don't want His anointing. We say, "Give me a man, marriage, alcohol, or drugs." Let me help you: Don't try to get rid of your emptiness. It was put there by God so He could fill it with His oil.

God wants to give this generation oil, but this generation doesn't want oil. This generation wants friends. Those in this generation can't handle being by themselves. We won't even drive in the car without the radio on because we don't want to feel alone. God put emptiness there as an indicator of our need for God, so we would call out to Him to be filled with His oil. How would you know your car needed gas or oil if the indicator light didn't show it was low?

I've learned a few things over the years.

First, those who are greatly used by God have become comfortable with emptiness. They know that God put emptiness there to help them recognize their need for Him. Without emptiness, they may never cry out, "God, I need You!"

Second, people who are greatly used by God are sometimes lonely. I know we don't like that. We want friends around all the time. But the more people we have around us, the less opportunity we have to hear God. God wants to talk to us, but He requires that we bring an empty vessel.

Third, I haven't discovered anybody who has been greatly used by God who hasn't also been hurt or betrayed. Mighty men and women of God get hurt just as everyone else. The difference is instead of going to God empty, most people take on the hurt themselves, piling fleshly things into their spirits—things such as offense, anger, and bitterness. Though these emotions feed the flesh, they also crowd the spirit, leading people to inadvertently repel the infilling of God. Even in these difficult moments, God gives the blessing of emptiness. I know it hurts, but you can take that hurt directly to God, have Him heal it, and be refilled.

My challenge to you: go to God first. Go to God hurt, worn, desperate, and empty. You increase your capacity for God to work miracles in and through your life when you do this. You should not be content with a little bit of oil. A little bit of oil runs out. You will not shift regions with a little bit of oil. You won't be able to speak to principalities with a little bit of oil. You will not see your family saved with a little bit of oil. The lame are not going to walk and the dumb will not talk with a little bit of oil. You need to go before God as empty as you can so you can be filled to the greatest capacity possible.

EMPTY = DEAD

In talking about emptiness, we're actually talking about death. There are several ways you can put to death the things that limit your capacity.

1. Nail them to the cross.

Galatians 5:24 says, "Those who belong to Christ Jesus have nailed the passions and desires of their sinful nature to his cross and crucified them there." Whatever it is in your life that is against God, whatever keeps you from experiencing God and walking in His ways, nail it to the cross. Addictions, pornography, and gossip—nail those to the cross.

2. Confess them to God.

First John 1:9 says, "If we confess our sins to him, he is faithful and just to forgive us our sins and to cleanse us from all wickedness." Confess, repent, and then go to Him boldly, empty and ready to be filled.

3. Surrender.

Romans 6:11–13 says, "So you also should consider yourselves to be dead to the power of sin and alive to God through Christ Jesus. Do not let sin control the way you live; do not give in to sinful desires. Do not let any part of your body become an instrument of evil to serve sin. Instead, give yourselves completely to God [surrender; be empty], for you were dead, but now you have new life. So use your whole body as an instrument to do what is right for the glory of God." Being used by God is not just connected to desire, but it is also connected to capacity. You can say you want to be used by God all you want, but if you don't surrender, your capacity to contain the oil of God is limited. Have you tried filling a container that is already full? It doesn't work.

Emptiness refers to being dead to sin. We say with our mouths that we want to be used by God, but do our lives show that we want to be used? Are we willing to pay the price? I've heard it said that there is not a man who has been used by God who has not first been bruised by God.

SHUT THE DOOR BEHIND YOU

In 2 Kings 4:4 the prophet told the woman:

Then go into your house with your sons and shut the door behind you. Pour olive oil from your flask into the jars, setting each one aside when it is filled.

Some people do things to look spiritual. They want everybody to see what they're doing. They want an audience for their gifts, anointing, or blessing. But the miracle realm doesn't work this way; it flows in secret. It flows out of surrender and humility. Most of the time the way God works is so counterintuitive that when we start out with Him, we'd rather keep it to ourselves.

Think about Naaman. He was a commander and mighty warrior in the Syrian army, but he was a leper. (See 2 Kings 5.) He was unclean, and in those times lepers were shunned and had to be separated from society. Naaman's story also seems to suggest that his condition was not widely known. If everyone knew about his disease, it would have been a deadly blow to his status in the kingdom.

But the king gave him provision to seek out the man of God for healing. But before he could receive his miracle, his ego had to be broken down to the point where he was humble enough to try anything. He had to be drawn into the secret place—a place away from the eyes of the people in the kingdom he served.

When Naaman sought out the prophet of God, nothing about the encounter was as he expected. The prophet sent a messenger with instructions for Naaman to wash in the Jordan River seven times, and after he did this, he would be made clean. At first Naaman was angry. He actually stomped away from the prophet's house with no plans to follow his directives. Naaman thought Elisha would address him formally and raise his hand in some dramatic gesture and call out to God to heal him. But Elisha did nothing of the sort. There would be no fanfare, no thunder from heaven, no one but God to see that he followed the instructions.

God used the peculiar nature of this miracle to humble Naaman. When Naaman finally submitted and obeyed the instructions the prophet had given him, he was healed. The Bible says his skin became as healthy as that of a young child. God's way of bringing healing was the opposite of what Naaman expected. God worked in secret, and He does the same today. God will only begin to work through you publicly when He knows He can trust you to obey what He tells you in private.

Unlike Naaman, the woman in 2 Kings 4 and her sons started in a place of desperation and surrender. Still Elisha said, "Shut the door behind you" (v. 4). Miracles are not born in public display but in private devotion. The power of God begins flowing in private.

A lot of people want to be used publicly but don't want to be bruised privately. Yet the anointing, gifting, or miracle is all for God to get the glory. It is not about anything we do, except that we come willing and empty. Yes, the woman had oil, but she did not know how it was going to be used. How did she handle that? Second Kings 4:5 says that "she did as she was told." She had her sons continue to bring jars to her. She had to have believed that God would do the impossible with those empty jars. The Bible doesn't show that she asked, "What am I going to do with these empty jars?" It says "she did as she was told." She kept pouring—behind closed doors—and the oil never ran out.

> Soon every container was full to the brim! "Bring me another jar," she said to one of her sons. "There aren't any more!" he told her. And then the olive oil stopped flowing.
> —2 Kings 4:6

The oil only stops when empty vessels stop coming. When we stop coming to God, that's when the oil stops. When we stop recognizing our need for Him, we stop coming. The issue is not God's supply. God's supply is limitless. The issue is our demand.

RESPOND

That we are not seeing the fullness of God's power in this generation has absolutely nothing to do with God's ability. God is just as miraculous and supernatural as He was at any other time in history. The Bible says He doesn't change (Mal. 3:6). This means that whatever you've seen Him do in the past He can still do. So why aren't you seeing His power in your life?

Is it possible that the only reason you've stopped seeing the oil flow in your life is because you've stopped asking for it? Is it possible that the oil stopped flowing in your life because you don't have an empty vessel to contain what God wants to do? Are you so full of yourself—your flesh, your desires, or pride—that there's no room for His oil?

Miracles are not born in public display but in private devotion.

In the widow's story the oil stopped when the empty vessels stopped. God *always* supplies oil when there is a demand. If you want to see God move in this generation, you need to understand this truth. Revival flows through us. I challenge you to ask yourself: Why is revival not happening in my life? Why do I not see miracles, signs, and wonders taking place in my generation, my home, or wherever I go?

The question is, Are you full, or are you empty? Is there room in your life for the anointing, for the presence of God? Is there anything in your life that is crowding out His ability to use you? Can He fill you with His oil? Is there anything keeping you from receiving the fullness of what He wants to do in your life? Even if you have a little bit of pride or a little bit of whatever, that little bit is enough to limit His ability to fill you completely.

God may be using you, and you may be anointed, but God wants to do more. When I get a glimpse of what God wants to do, I get excited. I become aware that whatever little bit of "stuff" I've been holding on to needs to go. We have to be careful not to get to a place where we stop coming to God. It could be that God gave you a word for somebody one time, and all of a sudden you want to be known as prophetess So-and-So. God uses you to pray for somebody one time, she says her headache is gone, and now you want to launch a healing ministry. You got it. You're anointed. But you stop coming to Him, and you stop praying and depending on Him as much. You may be able to look back at certain seasons of your life and say, "Man, God was really using me back then." God hasn't changed. His supply is still there. The question then is, Are you still coming to Him?

God wants to do immeasurably more than anything we've seen, and He is inviting us to go deeper. I don't want to attempt to speak for you, but I invite you to go to God with a prayer similar to this one, letting Him know that you are reaching out to Him again, but this time you want to be emptied:

> *God, I give You permission to go into every area of my life that does not line up with You. Examine my heart, thoughts, actions, deeds, relationships, interactions, addictions, pains, and struggles. Go in deep, and if You find anything that is hindering me from being filled to overflowing, take it out of me. I want Your oil to flow in my life. I do not want to be so full that I cannot receive Your oil. So God, I come. Empty me of everything that is against Your will and plans for my life. I come seeking to increase my capacity to house Your Spirit. God, fill me up.*

There will never come a time when you will not need to present yourself back to God as an empty vessel in need of His filling. Never. The oil stops when you stop presenting yourself before Him empty. Surrender is not a one-time event. Don't allow the enemy to trick you into thinking it is. Surrender is a daily, hourly, moment-by-moment commitment to say, "Lord, I want to be right with You. I need You." Your acknowledgment of your need for God is an emptying out of yourself. Nothing—not money, reputation, or friends—is worth more than having the oil of the anointing of God flowing in your life.

CHAPTER 6

NO SUBMISSION, NO POWER

You will receive power when the Holy Spirit comes
upon you. And you will be my witnesses, telling people
about me everywhere—in Jerusalem, throughout
Judea, in Samaria, and to the ends of the earth.

—ACTS 1:8

EVERYBODY WANTS TO walk in power. Everybody wants to
receive a word from God. Everybody wants to prophesy. But
we can't do any of it without being submitted to God. One
of the things we need to talk about more as we pray for God to
blow the winds of revival is submission to the Holy Spirit. We are
professionals at being good at everything but submission. We don't
like it. We don't like it when somebody tells us what to do, and that
includes allowing the Holy Spirit to lead us. The way the old folks
would say it is the Holy Spirit will help us walk right, talk right, and
live right. To let Him do that, we have to surrender.

The reason we have a generation confused about revival is because
there are many people who think like Simon the sorcerer in Acts 8.
They think they can exercise special privilege and shortcut the way
to receive supernatural power to carry out the works of Christ. They
would rather have the anointing than a relationship with God. Do
you know what that looks like? It looks like tongue-talking whore-
mongers, tongue-talking cussers, tongue-talking alcoholics, and
tongue-talking fornicators. They want the gifts but don't want to
submit to God.

The problem we face as believers is that we leave the world confused about what kind of power God possesses when His people
live the same way they do—sometimes worse. While we're talking
about revival and the power of God, the world is looking on, trying

to figure out how we have power but don't live right, stop gossiping and watching pornography, or come together and love one another. What kind of power is this that we are talking about?

The world is waiting on us to arise like real sons of God (Rom. 8:19). They need to see us walk in God's full power. We cannot expect to see a perpetual move of God if we don't have power, and we will have no power without giving ourselves completely over to God. We must be willing to say, "We'll go where You go. We'll take on Your identity. We'll take on Your name. We will lose it all to follow You." By doing this, we open the door to an authentic overflow of the power of the Holy Spirit.

You Will Receive Power...

In Acts 1:8 Jesus gave His followers a prophetic word about their future and destiny. He said, "You will receive power when the Holy Spirit comes upon you." This is a good word. I imagine there was a feeling of strength and victory attached to it as He spoke to them. We as believers today like to hear this part of the verse, especially in Spirit-filled churches: "Yes, God! I receive Your power." Next, Jesus says, "You will be my witnesses...in Jerusalem, throughout Judea, in Samaria, and to the ends of the earth." The disciples are still tracking with Him, as would we be. "Amen. Thank You, Jesus," I can hear us say.

What we are witnessing in this passage is the Lord prophetically speaking by the power of His Spirit over the lives of believers then and now. He was spelling out our destiny, which is distinctly different from a destination. This prophetic word in Acts 1 is about the arc of the life of a believer. In essence, He was saying, "What's about to happen in your life is going to be more powerful than you can imagine. The Spirit of God is going to come upon your life, and He is going to empower you to make you witnesses. He is going to give you a worldwide ministry, and you are going to go to the ends of the earth proclaiming My Word. I've called you to preach My gospel and to be My witnesses."

I can see it: Just as this word ignited a revolution in the hearts of

Jesus's followers that spread all over the known biblical world, I can see it having a similar effect in our churches today. The whole place would erupt. People would lift their hands and say, "My life is going to be great because God is going to greatly use me."

The world is waiting on us to arise like real sons of God.

But Jesus was only telling *what* would happen. He did not tell *how* it would happen or what it would take to get to this place of spiritual power. With every *what*, there is a *how*, and by now those of us who are praying for revival already know the *why*. The *why* fuels our prayers, the *what* gives us direction, and the *how* is the deciding factor for how far we'll go with God and how much we're willing to surrender to Him in this current season.

...BUT THERE IS A COST

There's a point as the Spirit reveals the full extent of Jesus's call to destiny where many of us may get quiet. What if Jesus told us that on the way to receiving power, we are going to lose friends and people are going to talk about us? What if He said we may lose our houses or our jobs? What if it comes to losing health benefits or our cars? What if our children start acting up or our family members don't understand why we don't do the same things we used to?

What if it takes all this and Jesus says, "I'm still going to use you"? Some of us would say, "You know, I'm good where I am." Others may say, "I don't know about that." But let me challenge you again with the words of Christ: "If you try to hang on to your life, you will lose it. But if you give up your life for my sake, you will save it. And what do you benefit if you gain the whole world but lose your own soul? Is anything worth more than your soul?" (Matt. 16:25–26).

What are you willing to give to be used by God in this hour? Is seeing God move worth more than preserving your status in society? Is seeing God move worth more than preserving relationships with friends and family who don't understand the call of God? Is seeing God move worth more than preserving the comforts of your own soul? This is a hard word. I know some of us may not be ready to face this, but revival is costly to the flesh.

But God reassures us in this: "I will never leave you nor forsake you" (Heb. 13:5, NKJV). "My grace is all you need. My power works best in weakness" (2 Cor. 12:9). He says, "Whatever I take you through, the Holy Spirit will remind you of the things I've said so when you are in a moment that seems incredibly difficult, you will prevail."

- -

Stories
of the River

Two of the hallmarks of revival are repentance and salvation. Even in what we think are the hardest cases, nothing is too hard for God. Our church is located not far from a street in our city that has been known as a hub for prostitution. There are several adult stores on that particular part of the street as well. We've seen fewer and fewer of those kinds of businesses over the years, but they're still present.

One Sunday a lady walked into church right off the street, having just sold her body for money. She literally didn't even clean herself up first. She had decided that she'd had enough of that life and was drawn by the Spirit of God to come to our church. When the invitation to surrender to Christ was made, she responded and gave her life to Christ on the spot. As we prayed for her, she was set free and delivered. She came back the next week like a completely different person and to this day has not gone back to that life of prostitution. It's happening!

- -

Get Used to Being Uncomfortable

When God calls you to do great works, you must be willing to give up whatever you need to release to make yourself available to Him. As a witness of His glory, you will not get to go wherever you want to go on your own time. You don't get to determine when you go. You don't even get to determine how you go. When God has a call on your life, your personal schedule is irrelevant. Proverbs 19:21 says, "You can make many plans, but the Lord's purpose will prevail." In other words, there's nothing wrong with planning, but the sovereignty of God's purpose trumps your plans. Because God needs you to be unattached to the cares of this life, when you get too comfortable with your plan, He will intentionally make you uncomfortable.

The sovereignty of God's purpose trumps your plans.

This is exactly what He allowed to happen in Acts 8. The Bible says:

> Saul was one of the witnesses, and he agreed completely with the killing of Stephen.
>
> A great wave of persecution began that day, sweeping over the church in Jerusalem; and all the believers except the apostles were scattered through the regions of Judea and Samaria. (Some devout men came and buried Stephen with great mourning.) But Saul was going everywhere to destroy the church. He went from house to house, dragging out both men and women to throw them into prison.
>
> But the believers who were scattered preached the Good News about Jesus wherever they went.
>
> —Acts 8:1–4

Saul (who later became Paul) led the persecution of believers, which was the catalyst for their being sent out to preach the good news. This is so uncomfortable for many to embrace, and it may be a hard word for where God is moving His body, so I'll say it again:

God caused Saul to persecute believers to send them out so His purpose would prevail. Jesus said in Acts 1:8, "But you shall receive power when the Holy Spirit comes upon you. And you shall be My witnesses in Jerusalem, and in all Judea and Samaria, and to the ends of the earth" (MEV).

On the surface that sounds amazing. The Holy Spirit is going to come. We will receive power and minister around the world. Most would say, "Sign me up for that." However, Jesus didn't say how it would happen, only that it would happen. If you've been walking with the Lord for a while, you can probably attest to the reality that we didn't know where our *yes* would take us and what our *yes* would cause us to go through.

Some of us might not have said yes so readily if we had known the cost. Jesus said they would be His witnesses in Jerusalem, Judea, Samaria, and to the ends of the earth. Acts 8:1–3 tells us that Saul's persecution of the believers caused them to be scattered to the regions of Judea and Samaria. So how did they get to Judea and Samaria? Persecution. At times God uses persecution to advance His causes.

Considering that God had no problem turning up the heat on the believers in the early church to see a mass revival come, you must understand that God will also make you uncomfortable. Are you feeling uncomfortable around the friends and family you used to hang with? Are you feeling the pressure of being tied to a nine-to-five job? Are they turning up the heat, telling you not to talk about God? I need you to understand that God is calling you out. He, not the devil, is the One causing the people and environments around you to feel strange. So stop rebuking the devil.

I am not at all telling you to quit your job, break up with all your friends, sell everything you have, and move to Tanzania. I am encouraging you to reframe how you see the challenges you are facing in the natural in this season. I am encouraging you to seek the face of God for clarity and direction. Because you have cried out and He has answered, He is taking you up on your commitment to surrender to

Him to see how far you are really willing to go. He is calling you to respond once again.

When Jesus released the word of destiny in Acts 1, He did not tell them that the way they would be built up in the faith, the way that they would be strengthened and empowered, was by the threat of death. He did not say, "You will receive power to be My witnesses, and how you're going to get that power is through enduring death threats." I think He knew that would have been too much all at once. He gave them the first part and allowed the Holy Spirit to lead them through the second part.

In Acts 8:5 Phillip—a layperson, a deacon in the church—was sent to Samaria, a most uncomfortable place for Jews. From Jesus's encounter with the woman at the well (John 4) and His parable of the Good Samaritan (Luke 10:25–37), we know that these two groups didn't get along. Still, the Lord caused Philip to go there and walk in the miracle-working power of God:

> Crowds listened intently to Philip because they were eager to hear his message and see the miraculous signs he did. Many evil spirits were cast out, screaming as they left their victims. And many who had been paralyzed or lame were healed. So there was great joy in that city.
>
> —Acts 8:6–8

Revival broke out in Samaria. Because of increased persecution believers scattered into areas where they were not comfortable, and God used them mightily. They received power to carry out the work of the Lord in areas where they may not have gone on their own and to people who may never have heard the gospel.

Looking closely at the Scripture, you will discover that most of Jesus's instructions for proclaiming the gospel were given for all believers, not just for those operating in what are known as the five-fold ministry gifts outlined in Ephesians 4:11 (apostles, prophets, evangelists, pastors, and teachers). This means every believer has been given the task of proclaiming the gospel everywhere because we can never know where revival will break out. We need to be surrendered and ready.

We need to be surrendered and ready.

Some of us are secretly hoping that when revival breaks out, we won't be called to someplace uncomfortable. But what happens when the Lord does just that? His intention is for revival to break out wherever you're sent and that when you begin to proclaim the Word of the Lord, people are saved, healed, and delivered from all the power of the enemy.

THERE ARE NO SHORTCUTS TO POWER

When the truth of the gospel is preached, deception is exposed and people are moved to choose between the truth and a lie. The Bible says:

> A man named Simon had been a sorcerer there for many years, amazing the people of Samaria and claiming to be someone great. Everyone, from the least to the greatest, often spoke of him as "the Great One—the Power of God." They listened closely to him because for a long time he had astounded them with his magic.
>
> —ACTS 8:9–11

The people saw how this man moved in supernatural ways, and they thought they were seeing God's power at work—until they heard Philip preach. "But now the people believed Philip's message of Good News concerning the Kingdom of God and the name of Jesus Christ" (Acts 8:12). The power of God present in Philip's teaching convicted their hearts with the truth, and they recognized that all this time they had been deceived. As a result, many men and women were baptized, including Simon.

When the truth of the gospel is preached, deception is exposed.

But Simon had a little bit more going on. He began to follow Philip because he saw the power Philip operated in. It seemed he was trying to figure out how it worked.

When the apostles of Jerusalem heard that the people of Samaria had accepted God's message, they sent Peter and John there to confirm the new believers and baptize them in the Holy Spirit.

> Then Peter and John laid their hands upon these believers, and they received the Holy Spirit.
>
> When Simon saw that the Spirit was given when the apostles laid their hands on people, he offered them money to buy this power. "Let me have this power, too," he exclaimed, "so that when I lay my hands on people, they will receive the Holy Spirit!"
>
> But Peter replied, "May your money be destroyed with you for thinking God's gift can be bought! You can have no part in this, for your heart is not right with God. Repent of your wickedness and pray to the Lord. Perhaps he will forgive your evil thoughts, for I can see that you are full of bitter jealousy and are held captive by sin.
>
> "Pray to the Lord for me," Simon exclaimed, "that these terrible things you've said won't happen to me!"
>
> —Acts 8:17–24

Unfortunately for Simon, God doesn't work this way. He was given an opportunity to repent, but that's not what he did. His asking the apostles to pray for him made it clear that he really had no intention of taking his new commitment to God to full relationship status. He wanted a quick route to the power, but he didn't want a relationship. He wanted the power without submission. He didn't want to lose anything. He didn't want to be humbled or made uncomfortable. He somehow wanted to do everything the apostles were doing, but he didn't want to submit to the lordship of Jesus. If we aren't careful, we may find ourselves in the same place.

Have you ever been awake late at night and caught one of those weight-loss infomercials? It's as if they come on one after the other. They try to sell you all sorts of things they say will change your body without your having to do much work. "Take this pill, and you'll automatically lose weight." "Wear this shirt, and you'll automatically get a six-pack." If we're not careful, we can get sucked into being part of Generation Shortcut. We try to think of ways to get what we want without doing the work or feeling discomfort. We do this with the things of God as well.

Some of us want the power of God without relationship with Him. We see someone operating in a powerful anointing, and we want what they have, but we don't want to go through what they've been through to get to where they are in God. No, this will not be us. We will do whatever it takes to see the power of God moving in this generation. I believe we will be a people who will accept the engagement ring. We will not reject what God has freely given us. We will not shortcut the process to receiving the power of God, thinking that it can be bought with anything we have other than our whole selves. We will be the generation that knows the power of God is freely given to those who submit to God, withholding nothing. Hear me: there is nothing you possess that can equal what He can give you. What He requires from all of us is a level of submission that says, "I belong to You."

GOD'S ENGAGEMENT RING

The Bible says the Holy Spirit (whose power we receive) is the confirmation that we belong to Jesus. This concept of confirmation is loaded with meaning. In Ephesians 1:13–14 (NIV) the Bible says:

> And you also were included in Christ when you heard the message of truth, the gospel of your salvation. When you believed, you were marked in him with a seal, the promised Holy Spirit, who is a deposit guaranteeing our inheritance until the redemption of those who are God's possession— to the praise of his glory.

The word *deposit* is translated "earnest" in the King James Version, both words coming from the Greek word *arrabon*, meaning "pledge" or "downpayment."[1] In context of the church being the bride of

Christ, we can extend the meaning to include the modern Greek word *arrabona*, which means "engagement ring."[2]

Building from the concept of confirmation and deposit, 2 Corinthians 1:21–22 takes it further into ownership: "He anointed us, set his seal of ownership on us, and put his Spirit in our hearts as a deposit, guaranteeing what is to come" (NIV). The Holy Spirit is God's promise of marriage to His bride, the church. He is a confirmation that we belong to Jesus.

> *The Holy Spirit is God's promise of marriage to His bride, the church.*

When someone puts a ring on your finger, it says, "I'm taken." When we submit to the Holy Spirit, we're saying: "I'm taken. No one else can have me. Nothing else can have me. Nothing else deserves my affection and attention. Nothing else deserves my worship. I'm taken. I belong to someone. I have given myself away." In traditional wedding ceremonies the officiant will ask, "Who gives this woman to this man?" But in the kingdom we give ourselves away.

Simon is an example of someone who came but did not have the right heart. He had no intention of fully submitting himself in relationship with God. Therefore God could not give him the gift and power of the Holy Spirit. God would not put a deposit, guarantee, or confirmation on Simon's choice because he was simply enamored with the power he saw operating in the apostles' lives. He wanted what they had, but he didn't want who they worshipped. This is the very definition of *prostitution*—trying to pay for something that should be given for free in the confines of a genuine intimate relationship. God illuminated the life of Simon the sorcerer to show us what happens when someone says he believes but doesn't want Him. Jesus knows why we come to Him, and because He gave everything He had to us, including His own life, He will not accept anything less than everything from us.

RESPOND

The Holy Spirit is God's invitation to submission. If you don't want to be submitted, you can't have Him or His power. We are crying out for a perpetual move of God, one that the world has never seen. I've told you it's happening, but where we have to go next is total and complete submission. God is challenging every area of our lives to get us to respond to this one thing: either we belong to ourselves, or we belong to Him. This is not a plea to do better or try harder. This is a do-or-die moment: submit to Him, or be powerless in this next season. It's your choice.

> *The Holy Spirit is God's invitation to submission. If you don't want to be submitted, you can't have Him or His power.*

If you dare to submit to God, I challenge you to join me in this short, but dangerous, prayer:

> *Holy Spirit, show me every area of my life that is not submitted to You, in the name of Jesus. Amen.*

Now let me forewarn you: Within the next couple of weeks there will be moments and circumstances in your life that will cause you to wonder where in the world they came from. Don't panic, and don't get mad at God. He will remind you about the prayer you just prayed, and He will remind you that He is with you. Do not doubt that you have made the best choice of your life. You have just opened the door to the supernatural power of God to flow through you as you step out as His witness. You also have received the greatest gift ever given to man—God's engagement ring. It is the guarantee from God that everything He promised will come to pass.

CHAPTER 7

URGENT ANTICIPATION

"Behold, the days are coming," says the LORD, "when the plowman shall overtake the reaper, and the treader of grapes him who sows seed; the mountains shall drip with sweet wine, and all the hills shall flow with it."

—AMOS 9:13, NKJV

I N AMOS 9:11–14 the prophet foretold the rapid growth and abundance of the first-century church. As we pattern ourselves after the example of Christ and the apostles, this passage represents something prophetic for that generation and this one. It's telling us that God is accelerating the time between when we plant the seed of the Word—indicated by the plowman—and when we will see a harvest—gathered by the reaper—of souls, spiritual blessings, and an outpouring of the goodness of God.

In ancient times during the regular farming season the plowman and the reaper were never together. Those who sowed seed did it in one season, usually summer, and those who reaped did it in another season, usually fall. There was time between. Yet the Lord is saying that the days are coming when both will be on the field at the same time—"the plowman shall overtake the reaper." That suggests He is not only accelerating the harvest; He is also increasing the abundance of it. *The Message* translates the promise this way:

"Yes indeed, it won't be long now." GOD's Decree.
"Things are going to happen so fast your head will swim,
one thing fast on the heels of the other. You won't be able
to keep up. Everything will be happening at once—and

everywhere you look, blessings! Blessings like wine pouring
off the mountains and hills."

—Amos 9:13

This is why I say with confidence, "There's more." Now I add to it,
"But we don't have much time. Things are going to happen quickly."
To keep up with what God is doing, we need to take on a posture
of urgency.

In John 4 Jesus had gone to Samaria to talk to a woman at a well.
At His specific appointment with her He began to reveal the fact
that salvation was getting ready to come to the Gentiles (vv. 21–24).
Though every other Jewish person would walk around the city of
Samaria, He had a specific reason for going there. Jesus spoke prophetically to the woman, telling her about her life. This moment
had such an impact on the woman that she went into the city telling
everyone what Jesus had said and done. "Come and see a man," she
said, "who told me everything I ever did! Could he possibly be the
Messiah?" (v. 29). As "the people came streaming from the village"
(v. 30), Jesus looked up at His disciples and said, "You know the
saying, 'Four months between planting and harvest.' But I say, wake
up and look around. The fields are already ripe for harvest" (v. 35).
What was He saying?

---

*Wake up and look around. The fields are already ripe for
harvest.*

While the disciples were trying to leave and worried about Jesus
getting something to eat, there was a much more urgent need—one
that surpassed any natural need or want, such as food or Jesus's
maintaining His reputation. Jesus was letting them know that it
was harvesttime. Even though He had just planted a seed in the
woman's heart, He also was reaping the harvest as the townspeople
came out to see who He was. He made the statement in verse 35 to
let them know that the normal period between sowing and reaping
had been accelerated—the plowman was overtaking the reaper.

There is an urgency in the spirit when times and seasons accelerate, because if we don't get busy with the harvest, it will spoil. Just as Jesus needed His disciples to understand this, we too need to get this sense of urgency into our spirits.

No one is talking about the urgency of Christ anymore. These days sermons are about "bless me," how to be a better this or that, or five steps to this and four steps to that. They want to talk about the latest movies and the most "relevant" thing in popular culture. I'm not against other people's preaching, but I remember a time when preaching seemed to be elementary. They kept it simple, and though some preachers may not have had the most scholarly grasp of the Scriptures, clever revelations, or full contextual prophetic understanding, they did have a relationship with Jesus and the urgent anticipation that any Sunday could be the last Sunday. They never took for granted that somebody might not have had the opportunity to hear about Jesus before he faced Judgment Day, so they would preach every week about Calvary, about the blood that never loses its power, and that Jesus is coming again. Now we have a generation of people who sit in church Sunday after Sunday and rarely hear of the blood and cross of Jesus—and we certainly don't hear about the Second Coming. To skip the central messages of the gospel is to preach as if we have time.

A Season of Acceleration

When Jesus entered the earth, acceleration began. The fulfillment of Amos 9:13 has been happening over the last two thousand years, but there are many who are unaware that Jesus's coming is near. In 2 Peter 3 the apostle Peter wrote about the last days to remind the believers that time was short. In verses 3–4 he said:

> Most importantly, I want to remind you that in the last days scoffers will come, mocking the truth and following their own desires. They will say, "What happened to the promise that Jesus is coming again? From before the times

of our ancestors, everything has remained the same since the world was first created."

In other words, people will say: "There's nothing different. Why are you preaching with such urgency? Everything is the same." They are forgetting that, according to the next few verses of 2 Peter 3, God intervenes in time and the affairs of men: "And by the same word, the present heavens and earth have been stored up for fire. They are being kept for the day of judgment, when ungodly people will be destroyed" (v. 7). If we believed this and kept it in our hearts, why do we think we have time? Peter went on to say, "But you must not forget this one thing, dear friends: A day is like a thousand years to the Lord, and a thousand years is like a day." In other words, since the day that Christ came as a baby until now, it's only been two days to Him.

Look at everything that has happened in two days. We are in a season of acceleration. To God, He just came. For us it may seem as though we've been waiting for a long time, but Peter assures us that "the Lord isn't really being slow about his promise, as some people think. No, he is being patient for your sake. He does not want anyone to be destroyed, but wants everyone to repent" (v. 9). Christ hasn't come back yet because He is gracious and merciful. He's slow to anger and patient. He could come right now, but He sees the condition of the earth. He sees that people think they have time, and in His mercy He's saying, "Not yet."

But the day is coming:

> But the day of the Lord will come as unexpectedly as a thief. Then the heavens will pass away with a terrible noise, and the very elements themselves will disappear in fire, and the earth and everything on it will be found to deserve judgment.
>
> —2 Peter 3:10

Those of us who understand the times and season, like the sons of Issachar, are praying, crying, and falling on our faces so much because we know that the revival God is bringing may very well be the last one. This could be the last one!

> *Every time we come together could be the last time. Every time we open our eyes could be the day. How will you be found?*

Some of us are confused, waiting on this or that to happen to signal the start of the last days because of varying eschatological beliefs. Others of us are in Matthew 24 and Daniel 10 with a calculator, trying to figure out how long we have left to sin before we get our lives right with God. The Bible says that "the Lord will come as unexpectedly as a thief" (2 Pet. 3:10). Even those who think they know will be surprised. Every time we come together could be the last time. Every time we open our eyes could be the day. How will you be found?

- -

Stories
of the River

I have a good friend from North Carolina. His name is Pastor Tony Jones. Tony is precious to our church because he flies in from North Carolina to Orlando every single month for our monthly Presence Nights. Unbeknownst to me, during one of the Presence Nights, Pastor Tony quietly placed on our church altar the name of one of his members who was battling sickness. We have a growing stack of papers on our altar, where people have placed the names of sick loved ones in faith. We've seen a number of people whose names were placed there miraculously healed.

Sometime later Pastor Tony asked me to minister at his church during their church anniversary, and I gladly accepted his invitation. The presence of God was strong that night as the people worshipped God. After I preached, there was a time of prayer, and the Spirit of God demonstrated His power among the people.

Pastor Tony asked me if I would pray for a precious lady who was dealing with stage IV lung cancer. She had been given just six months to live. As she came up, she was clearly weak from the medical treatments she received, and she was wearing a mask. As I prayed for her, I felt a tremendous heat, which sometimes comes when I'm praying for the sick, and I could sense the Holy Spirit working. With certain cancers there is usually not an immediate way to tell if anything happened, but I remember having a strong sense that something had taken place.

Months later I received a call from Pastor Tony about this lady. When she came to the service, she knew that nothing more could be done medically. The cancer had spread from her lungs to her neck and spine and was near the stem of her brain at that time. They were preparing for the worst, but Jesus met her that night. A few short months later, to everyone's amazement, her medical reports showed no sign of cancer! It's happening!

- -

A Special Announcement

Our cry for revival is not so our goose bumps can have goose bumps. We're not asking God for revival only so we can see more signs and wonders. It's not about gold dust, gold fillings, angel feathers, stigmata, anointed oil—none of that stuff. We are here in this moment because God invited us here. He walked into our space to make an announcement.

According to Micah 7, revival is a loud announcement, in the middle of corruption and scandal and sin, that the enemy's time is short. Our nation does not deserve revival. We have allowed the enemy to torment us with sin, scandal, and corruption. But our God is so merciful that He is sending revival anyway. He has put the enemy on notice that his days of ruling the earth are short. The more the fires of revival burn, the further out the enemy is driven. The closer God gets to us, the looser the grip of the enemy becomes.

Time is coming to a close. We should be living with urgency and expectation in our spirits. Any hour could be the hour. Any moment could be the moment. Any day could be the day. None of us has the time we think we do. But the less time we spend here, the closer we are to an eternity there.

God has withheld the second coming of Jesus so that those who don't know Him have an opportunity to accept Him. He could come right this second and judge the entire earth, and everyone who has placed faith in himself would be found guilty and on the wrong side of judgment. But everyone who has placed his faith in Jesus Christ would receive the gift of eternal life.

No preacher knows the day or the hour, yet we must preach with urgency. No prophet knows the time or hour, yet we must proclaim and prophesy with urgency. God has made a loud announcement, yet He exercises His patience. As Moses discovered, He is "the God of compassion and mercy! [He is] slow to anger and filled with unfailing love and faithfulness" (Exod. 34:6). Though we don't know the day, we must be grateful for God's great love and patience and wait with anticipation.

RESPOND

The Bible tells us that we are made right with God by placing our faith in Jesus Christ. That is true of everyone who believes, no matter who we are. This message has a twofold application:

1. If you are saved and have surrendered your heart to Jesus, you don't have more time to try and get yourself together. You need to live with urgency.

2. If you have never surrendered to Jesus Christ, you don't have the time to keep running. Today is your day.

What is amazing in both cases is that the Holy Spirit will reveal Jesus afresh to you. The best preaching can't do that. The Holy Spirit is the only One who can convince your heart of your need for Him. All you have to do is accept His gift of forgiveness and eternal life. You have the capacity to believe. He is taking the scales off your eyes, and the veil on your heart is being removed. Will you believe? Will you accept Him?

If you have said yes, pray this prayer with me now:

> *Lord Jesus, I'm not running from You anymore. I'm running to You. I believe that You are the Son of God, who died for my sins, and that God Your Father raised You to new life. I receive Your sacrifice and forgiveness.*
>
> *Today, I acknowledge that I need You. I surrender my life to You completely. I know I don't have time, so I pray that You will fill me with Your Spirit that I may have the urgency to cry out for revival. I want to see it. I want to be a part of the mighty things You will do in this season. In Your name, I pray. Amen.*

CHAPTER 8

STAY AND WAIT

Do not leave Jerusalem until the Father sends
you the gift he promised, as I told you before.
John baptized with water, but in just a few days
you will be baptized with the Holy Spirit.

—ACTS 1:4–5

O NE OF THE hallmarks of my life and of our church is that
we are relentless about waiting in the presence of God. It's
one of the things people often comment on when they visit
Deeper. We've adopted the belief that God is not in our presence;
we are in His presence. That distinction is critical to how we navigate our rivers (services). We don't rush through moments, wanting
to move ahead with our plans for the gathering. We wait until He is
finished with a moment. And then we wait until He directs us to the
next moment. Some of the most significant miracles that have taken
place have happened after the service was dismissed. Many times
we will dismiss the service to give people the opportunity to leave if
they need to, but often people stay. I've dismissed rivers before, only
to see a couple of hundred people continue to wait in His presence
for over an hour or more. We stay because we need Him. We wait
because there is nothing more important than Him. Many believe it
just isn't possible for people to wait in God's presence today, when
so many just want to be in and out of the church service. But the
Lord has consistently rewarded this posture of waiting.

As I mentioned previously, several of the most significant miracles that have taken place in our midst happened after the majority
had left. This has happened both during our weekly gatherings
and at our Presence Nights, which are monthly services specifically designed to give God room to move. We have no agenda at

our Presence Nights other than to come and be in His presence and follow where He leads. We want to flow with Him. At Deeper we've come to understand that scripturally rivers are often used as a metaphor to represent the Spirit of God. The Lord has directed us concerning our purpose and potential through Ezekiel 47, in which the prophet had a vision of a river flowing from the temple. Our Sunday morning gatherings and Presence Nights are marked by being in the river of God's Spirit and waiting for the current to take us where He wants us to go. We have learned to throw away our oars and put up our sails.

Isaiah 33:21 says, "But there the glorious LORD will be to us a place of broad rivers and streams on which no boat with oars shall go and on which no gallant ship shall pass" (MEV). On the river of God, boats with oars will not move. Oars represent human effort and strength, our ability to determine the direction and velocity of where we are going. On the river of God, the Spirit leads us, and we wait on Him to direct us. And we have seen and experienced amazing things as a result.

In July 2017 an entire day of services was dedicated to giving God thanks and praise for an incredible miracle He had performed for a family in our church. (I will share more about that miracle in chapter 9.) After the second service was over, as usual people remained in the sanctuary because we could still sense the presence of God. I decided to sit down in reverence when I felt a tap on my shoulder. I turned around, and a lady was standing there with a baby in her arms. The baby was four months old, and when I looked at her little body, it was limp, and she was in a somewhat catatonic state. The lady began to tell me that the Holy Spirit prompted her to come back in the church and not leave without having someone pray for this beautiful child. She explained that the child was partially brain dead, and the doctors said she would never smile, speak, or eat on her own. We prayed, and in an instant the baby's eyes focused and became normal. She smiled and began cooing and looking around, all things that she had never done in her young life. She was healed in an instant.

Another time there was a lady who had severe neuropathy. She utilized a walker and was partially blind. We prayed, and the Lord took away all her pain and restored her sight. Her husband came to the service carrying his wife; he left the service carrying her purse! The Lord healed another woman of lupus and rheumatoid arthritis the very week I sat down to write this. The arthritis had damaged her ligaments so extensively that her hands were shriveled up and contorted. As I took her hand in mine and began to pray, we literally watched her hand unravel like a flower bud opening to the sun. Jesus healed her and straightened her withered hands right in front of our eyes. She was astonished, and so were the people who were standing there. The Lord took away all the pain in her body.

Another young man had what doctors believed was nerve damage to his eyes and the early onset of glaucoma. When he opened and closed his eyes, the man felt excruciating pain and pressure. When he came to church, he was a little scared that he would completely lose his sight. We began to pray for him, and a heat radiated through his eyes, and he was instantly healed! The pain and pressure he was experiencing instantly left, and he was able to remove the special glasses he was wearing to protect him from light sensitivity. All these things happened after we officially dismissed. It seems as if something special is released to those who will embrace the posture of waiting.

Most of us know the Great Commission as the words Jesus spoke in Matthew 28:18–20: "I have been given all authority in heaven and on earth. Therefore, go and make disciples of all the nations, baptizing them in the name of the Father and the Son and the Holy Spirit. Teach these new disciples to obey all the commands I have given you. And be sure of this: I am with you always, even to the end of the age." But what some of us don't know is that, according to scholars, these words were spoken at the same time He declared the words of Acts 1:4–5.[1] As a matter of fact, He didn't say this just to the eleven; He also said it to the five hundred Paul wrote about in 1 Corinthians 15:6: "After that, he was seen by more than 500 of his followers at one time."

Now, looking at the totality of what Jesus was saying, we can understand that before they were to go and make disciples of nations, He was commanding all five hundred of His followers to wait to receive the power to do what He was commissioning them to do. This is important because sometimes we get excited about the revelation of the call of God on our lives and rush out before God can give us what we need to accomplish it. He is telling us, as He told the five hundred, "Before you go, I need you to stay and wait." What's interesting is that Jesus didn't tell them how long they were to wait. He just said, "Wait until…"

Not everybody could get with that. So the Bible reports that only 120 of the ones who were present to hear the Lord's command went to the upper room to wait, which means that 380 people didn't go, or maybe they went but didn't stay. Whichever way we look at it, it seems that the 380 lost their tenacity, which we'll talk about more in the next chapter. These 380 were the majority who decided, like many in this generation, they had something more important to do than wait. There is nothing in our lives more important than waiting on God. Those who stayed remained because they knew they needed what Jesus promised was coming. They all had the same passion, which is another way *homothymadon*, the Greek word for "one accord" in Acts 1:14 (KJV), can be translated. It comes from two Greek terms that mean to "rush along" and "in unison."[2] The 120 stayed because nothing else was more important to them. Inevitably there are always some who have another priority.

- -

Stories
of the River

There is a precious lady in our church who has a smile on her face every time I see her. Since she is always smiling, I was unaware that she was very sick. She had a cancerous tumor on her side the size of a melon. When I was told about her diagnosis, a righteous indignation rose up in me. I knew I wanted to pray for her the next time she was at a service.

One Saturday evening I read about Smith Wigglesworth and the miraculous healings that took place through his ministry, and I was struck by how bold he was. When I went into the service the next day, those powerful accounts were still reverberating in my mind.

That Sunday the atmosphere of worship and faith was electrifying, and I asked if this precious woman was in the room. She was present and came forward. A boldness came over me as the other leaders and I spoke to the cancer and the tumor and prayed for her healing. After we prayed, we felt a tangible sense that the Lord heard us and would answer.

The following week when she showed me the spot where the tumor was, I could feel that it had shrunk from the size of a melon to about the size of a golf ball. And instead of being hard, it was now soft. Today she says she can't even feel the tumor. On top of that, after losing a lot of weight because of the cancer, she's at a healthy weight again, and she's still smiling! It's happening!

- -

"I'M NOT LEAVING"

But there was a group of people who kept the posture of waiting. In essence, they said, "We're not going anywhere until we see it. We're not leaving until we receive it." We have the opportunity to duplicate this posture in this generation. Many already have. This is the posture of those who believe there is something the Lord wants to pour out, and they know He is only going to pour it out on those who will stay and wait. The experience of those who stay "until" is different from the experience of anyone else. Those who stay get God. The 120 of Acts 1 set a precedent. They decided they were not going anywhere until they received what they were promised, and they received God.

They didn't try to manipulate God to get Him to work on their terms. They submitted themselves to His timing.

The 380, on the other hand, either got distracted along the way or decided it wasn't worth it. Impatience and spirits of control arose in them, and they began to move out of their position, perhaps questioning the details of God's command: "How long are we supposed to wait here?" "What did He say was going to happen?" They sat there for a while, fifty days, the Bible says, and nothing happened. Maybe they left one by one, wondering, "What is this thing? What if it's not going to happen? Maybe it's not going to happen. Maybe I don't need this as badly as I thought I did. I have other things to do." The real question, however, is, What did they value more than waiting on God?

There's something about those who say, "I'm not leaving," whether it's Jacob, who said, "I'm not leaving until I'm changed," or the woman with the issue of blood, who grabbed the hem of Jesus's garment. They were not willing to let go once they grabbed hold of the promise. No matter what it cost them personally, they were going to hold on until they received what they had been waiting for. I can imagine that for the rest of Jacob's life, he was asked, "What happened to you?" I can also imagine that he was grateful to respond, "I got hold of God."

We ought to have such an encounter with the Lord that it causes people to ask, "What happened to you?" After the 120 received the Holy Spirit, amazing works of the Lord followed them. Miracles, signs, wonders, and salvations accompanied their experience. People who witnessed the events wondered, "What happened to them?" What happened is that they waited and received from the Lord. If you will stay and wait, you too will receive more of God. If you stay and wait, people will ask you what happened. And if you stay and wait, you will be able to say, "I got ahold of God because I wouldn't let go until I was changed."

WORTH THE WAIT

One thing we need to understand as we wait is that God does not move according to our time. He created time, and He holds it in His hands. So when God invites us into postures such as waiting, we should know the answer to questions such as "How long do I have to wait?" As we discussed, Scripture is clear. We wait "until." There is no time frame on that. As a matter of fact, some individuals didn't see the promises God made to them in their lifetimes. Think of Abraham and the many others in the Old Testament who "died still believing what God had promised them. They did not receive what was promised, but they saw it all from a distance and welcomed it" (Heb. 11:13).

But for us, when God has spoken something, we want God to manifest it within the next fifteen minutes, fifteen months, or whatever time frame we decide is reasonable. And if it doesn't happen in that time, we're discouraged.

> We ought to have such an encounter with the Lord that it causes people to ask, "What happened to you?"

We don't like to wait for anything. But what we need to know is that what God wants to give us is worth waiting for. Consider this: It takes seventeen to eighteen hours to build a Toyota,[3] but it takes four months to build a Rolls-Royce.[4] Part of the reason is because a Toyota is made by robots, and a Rolls-Royce is made mostly by hand. If a mistake is made in the manufacturing process, it's done ten thousand times with a Toyota but only once with a Rolls-Royce. And so, ultimately, if you want something of value such as a Rolls-Royce-level blessing, you will have to wait, and it will be worth it.

God has His hands on this generation, inviting us to get in the right posture to receive revival in our lives, homes, and community, and in the nations all over the world. And this is not a prefabricated move where a die has been cast. God is doing an original work in this generation for those who are willing to wait.

WAITING WHEN IT'S *NOT* HAPPENING

Most of the modern-day revivals we've seen in the world from the 1950s until now can be traced back to a room in Argentina.[5] In the late 1940s missionary Edward Miller had been ministering in the area and was not seeing results. Miller was frustrated. He had been going door-to-door, evangelizing people, doing tent meetings, and all the other things missionaries normally do, but nobody was showing up. It was the same story for all the missionaries in that nation at the time. It seemed that the heavens were closed over the region, as they were not making any progress. So over time many of the missionaries left, but Miller stayed.

Eventually the Lord invited him to do something: pray for at least eight hours a day. If you know anything about missionaries, you know that they raise money from donors to fund their efforts and provide them with basic living necessities. People do not necessarily send support so the missionary can stay in his room and pray all day. Donors want to know that missionaries are out among the people, witnessing and saving souls. Miller put all the expectations of other people on hold and accepted the Lord's invitation to pray. Of course, now you're probably expecting me to say the demonic oppression over the region broke and the heavens were opened. But as it turned out, nothing happened. He prayed and prayed and prayed, and nothing tangible seemed to happen. So finally he gave the Lord a deadline.

Don't judge him; we do the same thing. We may not be quite so bold as to tell God, "On January 1, I expect to see my breakthrough." But know that God understands our thoughts and actions that communicate the same thing. He knows when we have given Him an unspoken deadline because when He doesn't meet it, we stop calling the prayer line. We stop being specific in our prayers. We stop believing. We stop attending church. We lose our zeal. Whether we admit it or not, we gave God a deadline, and since He did not meet it, we stopped reaching out to Him.

So Miller gave God a deadline, but he verbalized it and said, in essence, "I will keep praying, but I need to see You do something by _____, or I will return to my usual missionary duties." He continued to pray eight hours a day as God had told him to do, and then the day of the deadline came. Miller grabbed a pocketful of tracts, but just as he was heading outside to pass them out, another local pastor showed up at his door. The two ended up talking for hours. The other pastor was hardly an encouragement to Miller; he had troubles of his own and was even more frustrated and discouraged than Miller was. Miller ended up encouraging the other pastor rather than receiving the encouragement he needed.

The other pastor had brought his unsaved son with him. As they were leaving, which was now well past his deadline, Miller asked the teenage boy a searching question. One word led to another until the boy began to weep. He ended up giving his heart to the Lord. Of course you would think this was the moment of breakthrough, that the Lord had finally come through for Miller. But that was not the moment of breakthrough. Basically all God said was, "I will bring them in when I'm ready. Go back and pray."

Faithfully Miller continued to pray eight hours every day. One day as he was praying, the Lord invited him to a new season. In the new season, God gave him this instruction: "I want you to do a prayer meeting in which you will pray every day from 8:00 p.m. until midnight. Invite people to join you. But whoever comes must commit to praying the entire time. If they will not commit to praying the entire time, ask them not to come."

So Miller did as instructed, and only a handful of people joined him in praying from eight to midnight. You're probably thinking this is when something happened, after they prayed. But no. They prayed and prayed and prayed, and at the end of that first night Dr. Miller asked, "Has anyone heard anything from the Lord? Does anyone have an impression?" One of the young women who'd been praying with the small group said, "I have this strange impression to go and hit the table in the center of the room. But it seems too foolish." It was so foolish to her, she couldn't even be persuaded to try it. So they didn't hit the table, and they all went home.

The next night, they came back, they prayed, Miller asked if anyone had heard from God, and everyone said no. Though the young woman had the same impression to hit the table, she did not pursue it because it seemed foolish. This cycle went on for three nights. Finally, after having the same impression, she agreed to try it once everyone in the room had hit the table first. They hit the table, one by one, and nothing happened. Then it was the young woman's turn. She went up and hit the table, and a physical rushing wind entered the building. Everyone fell to the floor in worship and began speaking in other tongues. They had an encounter with God, and the heavens were opened over Argentina.

Because this small group was faithful to obey God's instruction to wait despite the fact that nothing had happened for so long, He began to move. They opened a Bible school, and just a few years later a student who was walking and praying in the woods had an encounter with God that led to such a move of the Spirit they had to cancel classes for months. People could not stop crying. In addition, God gave the young student a prophetic word. He prophesied about different places that would have revival in the earth before the Lord returns. And would you know, every city he mentioned has seen one. All this is because some people were willing to stay in a posture of prayer and waiting.

WAIT, THE ANSWER'S ON ITS WAY

In Daniel 10 Daniel received a vision from the Lord that grieved him. He wept and went without food for three weeks. His posture was one of lament and intercession for what he saw concerning the future of his nation and the nations of the earth. Though the vision did not come with revelation, as it had in times past, he sensed that God wanted to do something. So for twenty-one days he did nothing but remain in the presence of God, praying for His plans to be revealed. Nothing happened for twenty-one days. And keep in mind, God did not tell Daniel that he would need to remain in this position for twenty-one days. When he embarked on this journey with the Lord, Daniel did not know how long he would need to intercede.

But on the twenty-first day an angel came and gave him the answers he'd been praying for. The angel said:

Daniel, you are very precious to God, so listen carefully to what I have to say to you. Stand up, for I have been sent to you....Don't be afraid, Daniel. Since the first day you began to pray for understanding and to humble yourself before your God, your request has been heard in heaven. I have come in answer to your prayer. But for twenty-one days the spirit prince of the kingdom of Persia blocked my way. Then Michael, one of the archangels, came to help me, and I left him there with the spirit prince of the kingdom of Persia. Now I am here to explain what will happen to your people in the future, for this vision concerns a time yet to come.

—DANIEL 10:11–14

The angel was saying that a heavenly decree had been made on the first day Daniel prayed, but the prayer had been held up. So he had to call Michael to fight with him so he could get the answer to Daniel.

In order for an answer to be released on the earth, it has to be given to someone who has jurisdiction in the earth. In order for a decree or an announcement to take root, it has to take root in the place where there is jurisdiction. There was a decree made in heaven, but it had to get to someone, in this case Daniel, who had divine jurisdiction over that region. In Daniel 11 we learn that because the decree was about Persia and the prince of Persia had no ability to stop it, he tried to keep it from being declared. He thought he could delay the answer long enough and outlast Daniel's ability to wait for it. But Daniel waited, holding a posture of intercession and fasting. The prince of Persia could not outlast Daniel's posture.

I need you to understand the power of waiting in this season. What the enemy was trying to do then and what he is trying to do now is hold up the answers to your prayers so you will get so frustrated you give up. But as with Daniel, God heard your cry on the first day. Some of you are getting frustrated because you believe that God hasn't heard you. But I want you to know that the moment you lifted your voice and began to cry out to God for understanding, the moment you lifted your voice and began to cry out to God for revelation, or the moment you lifted your voice to cry out for your son or daughter, your city or your nation, the Lord heard you. Though the enemy tries to hold up His response, God is releasing the answers to those who have found His favor.

I believe that we are in a season of breakthrough. This is a season when answers that have been held back for a long time are being released. The enemy knows he can't stop the decree. All he can do is fight its timing. Once the decree has been released in heaven, the enemy can only delay it. He knows that when it gets to us and we speak it, it cannot be stopped.

Psalm 2:7 says, "I will declare the decree of the LORD" (AMP). This means you need to agree with the Word of God—every single thing the Word says. You must speak the Word. You must speak the promises of God. Once you speak them, they will not delay. They will perform as God intends them to. They will not return to Him void.

One last amazing thing about Daniel's story: the spirit prince of Persia thought, "If I can hold it up long enough, perhaps he'll move." But the Bible says that when the angel found Daniel, he was in the same place. He never got off his face.

God is challenging you to hold your posture. Do not stop seeking God until you have received what He has promised. It will be worth the wait.

WE WON'T STOP UNTIL WE SEE IT

There is a statement that has gripped the heart of our church and has become a literal rallying cry for us in prayer: we won't stop until we see it! We are in a relentless pursuit for revival to continue not only among us but everywhere.

In 2 Kings 13 we see the circumstances surrounding Elisha's final prophecy.

> Now Elisha had become sick with the illness of which he would die. So Joash the king of Israel went down to him and wept before him, and said, "My father, my father, the chariot of Israel and its horsemen." Elisha said to him,

"Take a bow and arrows." So he took a bow and arrows.
Then he said to the king of Israel, "Draw the bow." So he
drew it. Elisha put his hands on the king's hands. Then
he said, "Open the east window." So he opened it. Then
Elisha said, "Shoot." So he shot. Then he said, "The arrow
of the deliverance of the LORD, and the arrow of deliverance from Aram; for you must strike Aram in Aphek until
you have destroyed them." Then he said, "Take the arrows."
So he took them. Then he said to the king of Israel, "Strike
the ground." So he struck it three times and stood there.
Then the man of God was angry with him and said, "You
should have struck it five or six times. Then you would have
stricken Aram until you had finished them. Now you will
strike Aram just three times."

—2 KINGS 13:14–19, MEV

In this passage King Joash went to Elisha and received prophetic
instructions to open the east window and shoot an arrow. Elisha
put his hands on the king's hands, and the king shot the arrow,
which was followed by the word that it was an arrow of deliverance
from Aram. Then Elisha told him to take the arrows and strike the
ground, and the king took the arrows and struck the ground three
times and stood there. The Bible says Elisha became angry with
him and said, "You should have struck it five or six times. Then you
would have stricken Aram until you had finished them. Now you
will strike Aram just three times."

*We won't stop striking the ground until we see revival in our
city, our nation, and around the world.*

Why would Elisha be angry that the king stuck the ground only
three times when he didn't tell him how many times to strike? The
implication here is twofold. First, the fact that the king struck the
ground three times and stood there could imply that he thought the
instruction was silly and didn't see the point. It's as if he were saying,
"What will this do?" How often do we do the same thing? If we

don't see the direct correlation or an immediate result, we question the effectiveness of continuing in prayer or fasting or believing and declaring. We do something a few times and then stand there with a posture of "Let's see if this does anything."

The second implication informs the posture we have taken at our church. He struck the ground three times, and Elisha was angry and said he should have struck it five or six times. The king stopped striking the ground after three strikes, but he was never told how many times to strike, which indicates he was to strike until he was told to stop!

The thought here is he didn't strike the ground with full confidence that it would bear fruit, so he stopped. How often do we stop before seeing full victory? Because of the king's actions Elisha told Joash that he would see only three victories. Had he kept going, his enemy would have been destroyed.

We've made a commitment to take the posture that we won't stop striking the ground until we see revival in our city, our nation, and around the world. Just because it's happening among us doesn't mean we can stop striking the ground. We are not after just small victories or a local movement. We are believing for a global outpouring, a global revival. We believe if it's happening anywhere, it can happen everywhere, and we won't stop until we see it!

RESPOND

God is looking for a generation that is willing to wait. Wherever you were when you received instruction or a promise from the Lord, go back to that place. When you first learned of it, did you pace the floor to see it manifest? If so, go back to that posture. Have you let your tears dry up? Open them up again. Have you stopped crying out to God? Open your mouth again. The Holy Spirit is telling me to tell you to go back. Go back to what you were doing. Don't leave your posture. Keep waiting. Keep praying. Keep believing. Keep fasting. It's happening!

Just because you don't feel it doesn't mean it's not happening. Just because you don't see the answer doesn't mean He hasn't heard you.

It's held up right now, but the answer is on the way. We are entering a season of breakthrough. I declare things that have been held up for a long time will break through for you, in the name of Jesus. The fight is about to be over, and the answer is about to be released. Stay and wait.

CHAPTER 9

CONTEND FOR THE
FLAMES OF REVIVAL

In the womb [Jacob] took his brother by the heel,
and in his maturity he contended with God.

—Hosea 12:3, nasb

G OD WANTS TO know how badly you want revival in your life and in your world. Have you reached the point where you are so comfortable with your life that you are willing to continue to contend with yourself and with man to get what only God can give? Would you believe me if I told you that there are some things that belong to you, that have always belonged to you, that you will have to contend with God for in order to see?

The difference between immature and mature believers is that the immature think their problem is people. The immature always think there is someone trying to keep them from their blessing. It's the immature who are always talking about haters. It's the immature who are always saying, "Don't let people do this," or, "Don't let people do that." For some reason or another they feel as if they are wrestling with men.

Mature people do not contend with other people. They are not worried about what other people think or say about them. They are not worried about how they look to others. And for those of us who haven't reached this place, this is the reason the church has not grown up. We have not been able to get to the place God wants us because we're still concerned about what the world thinks. We think that somehow we're contending with the world, and if the world likes us, then we'll be at a good place. But the things of God cannot be managed or dispensed through the systems of the world.

They can come only from God. There is a blessing with your name on it, and there is no man you have to wrestle with to get it. You will have to contend with God.

There is a blessing with your name on it, and there is no man you have to wrestle with to get it.

Contending with God is about posture. It's about how deliberately desperate you are to see the glory of God fill the earth. Will you contend with God for it? Will you press through the crowd to get it? Will you do whatever it takes to see it? The stories of Jacob, the woman with the issue of blood, and others who acted tenaciously throughout history will give you the faith to hold your position until you see what you've been praying for.

How Badly Do You Want It?

Somehow we've bought into a lie that God is going to grace us with His presence and everything we want if we just keep showing up. We act as if He is going to say, "Oh, OK. You have perfect attendance, so I'll just do something for you." But it won't happen that way. Where are the hungry? Where are the thirsty? Where are the desperate? Where are those who say, "I need You more than anything else. Nothing else matters. Nothing else will do. Nothing else will satisfy or satiate this thing I have on the inside of me because deep in my soul I am crying out for You"? God wants to feel our demand for His presence and power.

You're reading this book, and I'm saying, "It's happening." Maybe you've latched on to this truth as well and have begun to proclaim it in your own life. But I hope you are not missing the heaviness of the condition attached to having God move in your life. The question He is asking is, "How badly do you want it?"

I know you don't get the question right now. It's heavy. It has a condition attached to it. I believe we are going to continue to see increasing waves of revival come to our land. I believe that. But it's attached to a people who want it. How badly do you want it? What are you willing to do to get it? The pathway to revival will not get easier. There is no easy path to this.

God is saying this across the earth: Is there a people who want revival so badly they will do anything to get it? Are you willing to wrestle Me for it?

- -

Stories
of the River

One of the gifts of the Spirit that is in operation on a pretty regular basis at our church is the gift of words of knowledge. I, along with several members of our pastoral team, flow in this gift. One Sunday while I was traveling overseas, my friend Caleb was leading the services, and he often flows in this particular gift. The Holy Spirit gave him a word of knowledge about a person dealing with an issue with his or her esophagus that the Lord wanted to heal. The Holy Spirit then gave the church an instruction that to some might seem unusual, but I'm just going to tell you what happened that day.

The Spirit of God gave the instruction that we were to shout to the Lord in praise, and as we did, He would heal whoever had the esophageal issue. Having experienced so many miracles in our midst, our church did so in faith. Afterward a girl identified herself as being the one dealing with the esophageal issue. She said she felt something happen during the shout. Later she reported that when she got home, all her symptoms were gone. She had previously been unable to swallow, and in the midst of the praise that issue was completely resolved. It's happening!

- -

THERE ARE NO ACCIDENTAL MOVES OF GOD

There are moments when the Lord reveals certain things to us, enlightening our understanding and highlighting things for us. One evening as I was reading Luke 8, it was like the Lord put a neon highlight on the word *deliberately* in the following passage:

> As Jesus went with him, he was surrounded by the crowds. A woman in the crowd had suffered for twelve years with constant bleeding, and she could find no cure. Coming up behind Jesus, she touched the fringe of his robe. Immediately, the bleeding stopped.
> "Who touched me?" Jesus asked.
> Everyone denied it, and Peter said, "Master, this whole crowd is pressing up against you."
> But Jesus said, "Someone *deliberately* touched me, for I felt healing power go out from me."
> —LUKE 8:42–46, EMPHASIS ADDED

Through this story the Lord revealed to me that there are no accidental moves of God. We've heard stories of accidental wealth, where people win the lottery or receive unexpected sums of money through inheritance or a lawsuit. But these accidental millionaires don't tend to keep the money. Overwhelming statistics have been reported showing that within a few years some of the people who win the lottery, for example, are right back to where they were before the winnings. They are right back in the same financial straits because they squandered the money.[1]

A 2009 ESPN documentary called *30 for 30: Broke* looked at the myriad of athletes who had earned multi-millions of dollars over the course of their career and lost it within five years after their retirement.[2] Of course, these stories include people taking advantage of them and poor investments. Still, regardless of why they lost the money, their stories are heartbreaking. Yet they reveal the reality that anyone who steps into something unprepared or by accident—not with intention—will lose it. This is a revelation for all who want to receive the blessing, presence, and power of God in their lives, including you: that for which you are not prepared you will lose.

As I mentioned in chapter 5 while discussing empty vessels, God will only send what you have the capacity to receive. Think in these terms: the word *receive* can also mean keep, hold, or contain. God doesn't want people who have holes in their pockets to try to contain the revival He is sending. God is not going to send revival to a people who don't have wisdom to steward His blessings. In 2 Kings 4 we see how God worked through Elisha to bring miraculous provision into the widow's life, and we see how the oil only stopped flowing when the containers stopped coming. God is not short on supply. It is that He will not send what you do not have the capacity to receive.

God will not send what you do not have the capacity to receive.

May I suggest this? God won't waste revival.

God won't waste revival on a generation that wishes to happen upon the things of God by accident. He will not squander revival on those who won't create capacity for it. He won't waste revival on a generation that will say, "That was fun while it lasted." They desire to play in the gifts of God and lavish in the blessings, but when the fun and feelings are over, they're on to the next thing. "On-to-the-next-thing" people will not experience revival. What we create capacity for is what we will receive. If you stop creating room for it, it will stop flowing.

True revival doesn't happen by accident; it is deliberate. If I'm going to experience God, it's not going to be by accident. If I'm going to experience God, it's not going to happen by being random. Once I know who He is and find out I have access, my actions will become deliberate.

WILL YOU CONTEND WITH GOD FOR IT?

This is a lesson for the mature in Christ. Will you hear it? The Bible says Jacob matured, not because he wrestled with man but because he contended with God. We know the story of Jacob and how it was prophesied that though he was not the firstborn, he would still be blessed. We also know that from the womb Jacob contended for the blessing in his own strength by grabbing the heel of his twin brother, Esau, almost as if to fight him for the position of being the first one out. He didn't know the blessing was already his.

In the next and most notable instance, Jacob propositioned his brother at a weak moment to sign over his birthright to him. Jacob was used to working in his own strength—manipulating, lying, and stealing—for the things God had promised. Esau was so angry at Jacob that he wanted to kill him. Rebekah, their mother, told Jacob to flee to her brother Laban's home. Jacob had a whole other set of issues during his fourteen-plus-year stay there: Laban treated him badly, changed his wages ten times, and gave him the wrong daughter to marry.

God finally gave Jacob favor and released him from serving Laban, but Laban came after him. Running from Laban, Jacob had nowhere to go and thought about going back home. Then he remembered the broken relationship with his brother. In an attempt to mend the relationship, Jacob sent his family ahead of him, along with some gifts, to meet Esau. He hoped this gesture would soften Esau's heart. But for Jacob to live at peace with Esau, he needed to first make peace with God.

Left alone in the camp, Jacob was so restless he couldn't sleep. A man, the Angel of the Lord, God Himself, came and wrestled with him all night. (See Genesis 32:22–32.) In the moment when He came and tested him, God knew Jacob's destiny. He knew Jacob was used to fighting and getting his way. Though He wrestled all night, God had something else for Jacob. God took the struggle to another level when He reached out and touched Jacob's hip socket. I don't know if you have ever had anything dislocated in your body. I can only imagine.

When you watch sports, you can see people getting their fingers or shoulders dislocated, but a hip? The Bible says Jacob still didn't let go. Jacob made the more painful decision. Most of us, when we're hurting, let go of God to deal with our hurt. We get a little upset when bad things happen, and we recoil. We say, "Hey, I'm not going to come to church for a little while. You're not going to see me for a minute. I have to deal with some stuff. There are some things I need to get over." We let go. But God wanted Jacob to see what it takes to really press through to see a change. God wanted Jacob to show how badly he wanted it. "Do you want it so bad," God's actions may have suggested, "that even if I touch your hip socket, even if I allow pain in your life, and even if the pain results in a physical or emotional scar or handicap you have to live with for the rest of your life, you will still hold on?"

Jacob made the more painful decision—he held on instead of letting go. He held on instead of letting go to fix it himself. He chose to hold on to God because he knew God had something for him that was greater than all he had fought for up until that moment. So he cried out, "I will not let go until You bless me! I will not let go until I see, hear, experience, walk in Your blessing." So God said, "OK. You want change so badly? Here it is. Since you contended with Me, I am going to give you the blessing that was meant for you from the foundation of the earth. I am going to change your name so that everyone who sees you will call you by a new identity. But I am going to leave you with your limp."

Jacob matured, not because he wrestled with man but because he contended with God.

Some of us are so frustrated with God because He won't remove certain things from our lives, but that limp is the testimony. It is the thing you have to prove that you've been with God. It's the visible thing that others will ask you about, and you can say, "There was a day when I used to depend on myself. There was a day when I used to think I could do it myself, when I thought my method of movement was good enough. But then I met Jesus, and though He afflicted me, He also kept me. I walk with this limp so I won't forget to lean on Him. It's my testimony."

Jacob saw revival that night in the wilderness. All his life he fought to bring revival in his life through his own striving; he contended with Esau and Laban and any other circumstance that stood in the way of the promised blessing. But it wasn't until his encounter with God Himself that his fighting spirit was brought to its knees.

Every encounter with God changes you. It is biblically impossible to have an encounter with God and stay the same. But it's the desperate who hold on through the encounter no matter how painful it gets, who show God that they are willing to go wherever, do whatever, give whatever, and pray whatever to see it. Jacob showed his desperation. He showed how badly he wanted it. Now it's your turn to answer: How badly do you want it?

DELIBERATE DESPERATION

Certain rhythms and patterns in our lives unlock things in the spirit. God is a God of order, systems, and patterns. He intends for us to do certain things to see His power become active in our lives. He highlights one of them in the story of the woman with the issue of blood in Luke 8. In the midst of a mass of people pushing and bumping against one another, one woman did something different from everyone else, and Jesus noticed it immediately. "Someone *deliberately* touched me," He said. One of my best friends, Jason McMullen, who is the executive pastor at our church and the closest thing to a brother this only child will ever know, said it this way: "The deliberate will see a demonstration." I'll add this to it: the random will sometimes see relief, but the deliberate will see a demonstration.

"The deliberate will see a demonstration." —*Jason McMullen*

If there is anyone I know intimately who has walked out this truth, it is Jason. One of the most significant miracles I've ever heard of and certainly ever experienced took place for his family. The testimony of this miracle will be its own book one day, and it is one that will cause me to thank God for the rest of my life. Each of us who was there has his or her own perspective of this massive miracle. On the evening of July 3 I received a call from my friend and brother Jason asking me to pray because he was on the way to the hospital with his wife. At the time she was carrying their ninth child and was thirty-one weeks into the pregnancy. Their ten-year-old son had called Jason and said, "Dad, you need to come home because something is wrong with Mom." Jessica, his wife, said she wasn't feeling well. She had a severe headache and body aches, and she was vomiting. When asked about her level of discomfort, she said it was at ten. Jason later said that if any woman who has already given birth to eight children says her level of discomfort is a ten, you need to get her to the hospital.

Jessica knew something wasn't right, but she mainly wanted to make sure that the baby was OK. When they arrived at the hospital, the doctors initially didn't find anything wrong and were going to send her home. But she knew something wasn't right. They did further tests and concluded that she had spinal meningitis. Jason called to update me so we could continue to pray, and he told me at the time that they were going to be moving her to a different hospital that would better be able to care for mom and baby.

As Jason was gathering their things to meet Jessica at the other hospital since she was being transported by ambulance, one of the nurses approached him. The nurse asked him if he could walk him to his car. As they walked, the nurse told Jason that he was a believer and was praying with them. He then proceeded to tell Jason that while the initial diagnosis was spinal meningitis, he saw the doctors checking for something else far more serious: an amoeba.

An amoeba is a microorganism that can live in fresh water in subtropical climates whenever the water temperature rises above a certain point. An amoeba eats your brain. The average life expectancy of someone who gets an amoeba is between three and five days, and the mortality rate is 97 percent. The nurse told Jason he wanted him to know what they were possibly dealing with so he would be able to pray. Upon learning of that possibility, Jason called me so I could believe God with him. Around midnight I received another call from Jason saying that the doctors confirmed that his wife had an amoeba. When he arrived at the hospital, he learned that his wife was in the neurocritical ICU, and he was greeted by a team of doctors ranging from infectious disease specialists to an OB/GYN.

They told Jason that his wife had a 3 percent chance of survival and that they needed to give her a medicine so powerful it might kill her, but if she did not receive the treatment, she wouldn't survive the amoeba. Jason is a man full of faith, so upon learning the news, he brought the doctors together to pray for wisdom, healing, and direction. After they finished praying, he was also told that they needed to immediately deliver the baby because the baby wouldn't survive the medicine or the amoeba while in the womb. They then began asking about the other eight children, since they all had visited the same lake where it was believed Jessica contracted the amoeba. When Jason called home to ask about the other children, two of them were exhibiting the same symptoms as Jessica, so they were immediately taken to the hospital. After being tested, both were diagnosed as having the amoeba.

By the next morning two of their nine children had been diagnosed as having the amoeba; five of their children were in the hospital under observation, with the doctors expecting them to also test positive for the amoeba; and their newborn, delivered via C-section the previous night, was in the NICU. Jason's wife and eight of their children were in the hospital, with two of his children and his wife being given a 3 percent chance of living and a life expectancy of three to five days. The doctors wanted to place Jessica and the two children who had been diagnosed with the amoeba in an induced coma, lower their body temperature, and drill a hole into their heads to administer the medicine.

We were praying the entire time. I knew we needed to pray around the clock, so I didn't sleep that night. I stayed up to pray. I remembered a time prior when Jason asked me if I thought God had given me the gift of healing. He jokingly said, "It's not like the rest of us feel heat every time we pray." At the time, that was something I had never considered. But as I was up praying for Jason's family, I remembered that conversation, and I said, "God, if You have truly given me the gift of healing, please use it now."

The next day I met Jason at the hospital. I remember the peace he had; it was a peace that could only come from God. At one point he looked at me and said, "This must be happening so that God can get the glory out of this!" We spent time going back and forth visiting all of the children and Jessica and praying. Jason would often retreat to the chapel to pray and cry out to God for his family. He would not relent in his faith or waver in prayer. Neither did we. The details of what took place will become its own book, but I can tell you that God responded to our prayers. Almost as suddenly as the entire ordeal began, a miraculous thing took place. A nurse whom they had not seen or interacted with prior to this moment sat down on the edge of the bed and casually said to Jason, "Have you heard? No amoeba!"

Twenty-four hours later all six children were sent home cleared of the amoeba. No coma, no medicine, no hole drilled into their heads. A week later Jessica was home. No amoeba, no hole drilled in her head, no powerful medicine to kill an amoeba. As I am writing this, we are not aware of another case in the recorded history of the United States where this particular sickness was healed without medicine!

The baby is also home and is completely healthy. We serve an awesome God! The enemy intended to have seven caskets at the front of our church and for the national news to broadcast a story about how an entire family died due to a rare brain-eating amoeba. But the Lord turned our potential mourning into dancing and our potential sorrow into joy. We have living, breathing miracles among us every week when the McMullen family comes to church. It's happening!

When you randomly go through your life, sometimes you bump into relief because God is just that good. But the deliberate will see a demonstration of the power of God. There is a difference between being around Jesus and experiencing Him. Desperation can lead you to deliberate action that leads to seeing a demonstration of God's power. Those who stay in the posture and passion of consistently seeking God with desperation will see Him move in the deliberate way He intends.

The Bible says, "A woman in the crowd had suffered for twelve years with constant bleeding, and she could find no cure" (Luke 8:43). It goes on to tell us that this woman had run out of options and money trying to address this issue of hemorrhaging. She had done everything she could possibly do to be healed, set free, and delivered from this thing. And because the issue caused her to be labeled unclean, it had also become an embarrassment to her.

Then she heard that the healer was passing by. With large crowds surrounding Him, she had to make a life-or-death decision: "If I go out, knowing that I'm unclean, and He doesn't heal me, I will be killed. But if I stay in and keep bleeding, I will die." She was in a desperate situation.

Desperation is accompanied by corresponding action and can go a couple of ways, as I've already pointed out. Desperation can lead you to unwise decisions, or it can lead you to the right destination. Desperation, in the case of this woman, led to deliberate actions that led to the right destination. Sometimes God creates situations for you to understand that He's the only One who can change it. He's the only One who can fix it.

So in her desperation the woman chose the deliberate action of facing the large crowd and taking a chance on the Healer.

DON'T BE AFRAID TO REACH OUT AND GRAB IT

Pressing her way through the crowd, touching people despite her uncleanness, she came up behind Jesus, reached out, and touched the fringe of His robe. Immediately the bleeding stopped. The Bible does not say she tapped Him on the shoulder or called out and waited for Him to take notice of her. I imagine that, at some level, two things could have happened. One, her shame started speaking so loud that she felt too low to draw any attention to herself. She probably didn't have the confidence to stand up and look Him in the eye, so she reached out and grabbed His garment. Two, He was passing by, and she thought that if she did not reach out and grab of

Him what she could, she would miss her chance and not be healed that day.

How many of us will almost miss our time because we're afraid to reach out and grab hold of Him. At some point our situation will become so dire that, like the woman, we will resolve within ourselves to say, "I don't care what they say. I don't care what it looks like. I don't care if they talk about me. Jesus is about to pass by. I cannot let this moment go! I can't let this moment pass me by! I can't let this season pass me by! I can't let this word pass me by!" If God is doing something, if revival is happening anywhere, it can happen everywhere. We should be desperate enough to want it to happen to us. We have to reach out and grab Him deliberately, and He will know someone stepped out and did something different.

Jesus said, "Someone deliberately touched me." Peter was wondering how in the world Jesus would have noticed with all the people pressing in around Him. I can imagine Peter thinking, "All these people around? All the people who are associated with You? All these people who name Your name? All these people who go to church and lift up their hands? All these people who are singing these songs? All these people who show up every week? Jesus, don't You know that this church has twenty-five thousand people attending services every weekend?" But Jesus is saying, "Somebody is reaching out on purpose! Somebody has such a need that it is drawing something out of Me."

We're not going to accidentally enter revival. The Lord is literally saying to us, "Who is willing to be desperately deliberate?"

THE DELIBERATE ARE A TENACIOUS BUNCH

In addition to contending with God and not with man, another quality of a mature believer is tenacity, the ability to maintain a level of endurance and patience during difficult times. The apostles praised the Thessalonian church for this attribute: "As we pray to our God and Father about you, we think of your faithful work, your loving deeds, and the *enduring hope* you have because of our Lord Jesus Christ" (1 Thess. 1:3, emphasis added). This group of believers endured affliction and persecution and still are shown as examples of those who "remained strong in [their] faith" and "firm in the Lord" (1 Thess. 3:7–8). The entire narrative of Scripture would be completely different if it were not for groups of people who were tenacious in their pursuit of God. There are so many stories that would be different if it were not for the tenacity of the people who lived them. We have these stories to show us how we are to live.

Even in more contemporary history, our nation would look different if it were not for people who were tenacious. Every age has a tenacious group of people who will not give up easily. Think about the civil rights movement of the 1950s and 1960s. Civil disobedience through nonviolence took tenacity. It took tenacity for Elizabeth Eckford to enter Little Rock Central High in 1957 shortly after segregation laws had been overturned. Moments such as that one, captured in an iconic photo, are a testament to the tenacity of those determined to see black Americans have access to the same opportunities available to others. As a father of two girls, I don't know that I could send my daughters into the kind of hostile environment Eckford entered that day.[3] Then there was the 1960 sit-in at the Woolworth counter in Greensboro, North Carolina. Four African-American college students sat down at the lunch counter to protest the denial of service to black diners. They knew they were about to be beat up, arrested, and thrown into jail, but they had the tenacity to say, "We're doing this anyhow. We will not be denied what we know is possible."[4]

More famously, Rosa Parks chose not to give up her seat on a bus in Montgomery, Alabama, also showing a tenacious attitude. Some of you reading this book lived through times like these. Those now iconic moments were part of a larger pursuit of equality. The tenacity of the people actively and deliberately seeking what they knew was theirs sparked a worldwide revolution. From India to South Africa, oppressed people joined together saying, "We're going after something noble, something that should be for all people, and we're not going to stop until we get it." Each of these moments fueled the momentum for something greater. These were tipping points for single communities that became catalysts for other movements across the country and around the world.

THE TIPPING POINT

In his book *The Tipping Point*, Malcolm Gladwell defines *tipping point* as a series of consistent things that leads to the overflowing. So from this concept you wouldn't be able to point to one specific thing that caused another thing to happen, but the consistency of a set of actions can lead to an overflow. One drop of water from an eyedropper into a glass is not the catalyst for the glass overflowing, but consistently dropping the water in the glass can fill it and cause the water to run over. Considering the tipping point for revival, you never know what your next hallelujah will do. Or what your next "Thank You, Jesus" will do, or the next time you lift your hands or give an offering. You would not be able to say it was this offering or that praise that led to revival. It's the consistency of all the parts that leads to a tipping point.

Even the fight for civil rights in the fifties and sixties didn't start in the twentieth century; it began the moment people were oppressed. It just so happened that, because of several different factors, it came to be a catalyst moment in the fifties and sixties. People who were not connected with the terrible state of how certain people were treated were suddenly forced to take notice.

So it applies that once revival breaks out somewhere, it causes people, bit by bit, to take notice of what's happening until the ripples are felt everywhere. Once revival breaks out somewhere, it causes people everywhere to take notice of what's happening. And the response will vary. On one hand people may feel revival is not for them. They're not that desperate. They're not hungry. Others may say, "I need to change. I see what's happening with them over there, and I want that for my life." They may be encouraged to return to the place they had been before, but they feel that tenacity rising in their spirits, challenging them to contend for more.

Keep Asking, Keep Knocking, and Keep Seeking

Based on what I saw the Lord do in my third year of pastoring Deeper Fellowship Church, I am calling out to all who want to see revival. Do not be the generation that says, "If at first you don't get an answer right away, it must not be God's will." To see the blessing of God fall on this generation, we will need to be desperate enough to contend with God and deliberate enough to reach out and grab hold. The principle of the tipping point does not align with how we approach things these days. We are not going to go from one methodology to another. We are going to press in and hold our posture before the Lord.

Just like the woman in Luke 8 who saw a window of opportunity to be healed, tenacity causes us to see moments of opportunity that others don't see. It's easy to overlook something when you aren't searching for it. The tenacious are constantly seeking, knocking, and asking. When God spoke to the prophet Jeremiah and said, "You will seek Me and find Me, when you search for Me with all your heart" (Jer. 29:13, NKJV), contextually, He was saying, "I'm going to create a circumstance or an environment that literally causes you to look for what you weren't looking for previously. And when you look for it, you'll find it." Jesus said it too: "Ask, and it will be given to you; seek, and you will find; knock, and it will be opened to you. For everyone who asks receives, and he who seeks finds, and to him who knocks it will be opened" (Luke 11:9–10, NKJV).

For the believer, this posture is the essential, perpetual internal posture. Living from this place is key to continual momentum. It is the fuel of the engine of revival. Tenacious pursuit and perpetual seeking are the evidence of believers' recognition of their need for God.

Respond

From the beginning of your life until now there is evidence of the Lord's random acts of love and kindness toward you. Maybe you have not desperately or deliberately pursued anything from God. Or perhaps you've seen the power of God displayed at churches you've attended, and maybe you've felt His presence in a tangible way. Maybe the word of the Lord has been spoken, and you know that God has pronounced a blessing over your life.

In all these things maybe life has gotten in the way. Maybe you've been hurt. Maybe difficulties have caused you to lose a level of faith, hope, and expectancy, and you have been reduced to fighting for only what you can achieve in your own strength. Well, I want to tell you that a greater demonstration of God's moving in your life is coming, but only the deliberate will see it. I don't know where you are in your walk with God, but regain your tenacity. I don't know where you were when you were most passionate, but find that place again and determine in your heart, "I will not be afraid to reach out, grab hold, and not let go until I see it."

Chapter 10

A WORTHY HOST

When David returned home to bless his own family,
Michal, the daughter of Saul, came out to meet him.
She said in disgust, "How distinguished the king of
Israel looked today, shamelessly exposing himself to
the servant girls like any vulgar person might do!"
David retorted to Michal, "I was dancing before
the Lord, who chose me above your father and all
his family! He appointed me as the leader of Israel,
the people of the Lord, so I celebrate before the
Lord. Yes, and I am willing to look even more foolish
than this, even to be humiliated in my own eyes!"

—2 Samuel 6:20–22

WHETHER WE ADMIT it or not, we like to be in control of every aspect and moment of our lives. It stresses us out when we are not in control. Some of us even hate surprise birthday parties, a moment set aside to celebrate us, because we're not in control. Early in ministry, before I became a pastor, the Holy Spirit began to teach me about losing control, and what I have discovered is that if I am in control of every aspect of a service, He isn't. People have even said, "You're the most patient worship leader I've ever seen." When most people would move on or sit down, when the chorus seems to go a little too long or we're just standing there, I have learned that it is actually OK for us not to know what's next. For those of us who lead in some capacity, whether in a church or in the marketplace, it seems that we are expected to always know what to do. But we don't always know. Some people are willing to allow the moment to evolve. Others are not willing to wait and will take decisive action to push the moment along.

Have you been in a service that's going one way, and suddenly the pastor shifts to something else? This may have happened because they didn't know what to do, so they took it back to what they knew. What if God wanted to do something brand new, something beyond what they had ever experienced? What if God wanted to open a portal to something on the other side that was far greater than what they had ever known before? What if they released control? What if we do?

PROGRAMMED TO DEATH

I had a dream years ago about the same service that ran twice. I was ministering, and all these powerful and amazing things were happening. I came off the platform and thought, "Wow, God, that was amazing! You really moved. Thank You, Jesus." He said, "Let Me take you back and show you what would've happened if you had yielded to Me." The service played again, this time with God guiding me through all the moments when He could have done more. In comparison to the things He showed me when the service replayed, I would have never called what I experienced in the first service a move of God.

Many of us go to church and come home week after week saying things such as, "Man, wasn't that powerful? Didn't God move?" Yet we remain unchanged. May I submit to you that it is biblically impossible for you to have had an encounter with God without change? Everyone who has a genuine encounter with God always leaves different. Jacob left with a limp. The first Saul left with a crown. The second Saul left blind and with a new name. If you search throughout Scripture, you will find that every time someone had an encounter with the living God, that person was changed. That is why I wonder what's happening in our churches when we say God was there, but we're the same. Either it is an indictment against God, or we're lying, because now we're telling people that being with God doesn't make us any different. What can we say to the person who has fallen away when he says, "I've tried Jesus, and He doesn't work for me," if we've never had a genuine encounter with God?

A dividing line is being drawn down the center of the body of

Christ. On one side are those who have learned to do church without God. On the other side are those who are dissatisfied with doing church without God. We've been programmed to death. We've been told this is how long you're supposed to stay, this is how long you're supposed to sing, and this is how long you're supposed to pray. We even advertise how quickly we can do all these things: "Come here for the fastest one hour of church, and you'll be released right back into your life," as if God is not someone who's to be honored and worthy of whatever time it takes to engage with Him. "Come to a prayer meeting. It's only an hour long." Yet in the midst of our perfectly timed services, God is inviting us to a new place. The question is, Who wants to go?

THERE IS A WAY

In the days of Moses, God had graced His people with His presence in the form of the ark of the covenant. He had given them specific instruction on how to honor and protect His presence. But then they made a grave mistake and took the ark into battle against the Philistines. (See 1 Samuel 4.) Israel lost the battle badly. The Philistines captured the ark and took it back to their territory, but since they were not in covenant with God, they suffered curses instead of blessing, so they brought the ark back to the Israelites. (See 1 Samuel 6.)

For twenty years the ark of the covenant, which, again, represents the presence of God, was kept at Abinadab's house. (See 1 Samuel 7:1–2.) During that time neither the king of Israel—Saul—nor the people inquired after it. They didn't seek to honor, fear, worship, or tend to the presence of the Lord the way He was used to. Revelation 4 gives us a picture of what kind of eternal and ongoing worship God is used to in heaven—heavenly beings saying "day after day and night after night…'Holy, holy, holy is the Lord God, the Almighty—the one who always was, who is, and who is still to come'" (v. 8).

When David ascended to the throne, he decided he could not live without the presence of God. So in 2 Samuel 6 the Bible tells us that David gathered thirty thousand of his most elite troops to bring the ark to him. It was a clumsy acquisition. Because he was thirty years old when he finally took the throne and the ark had not been central to life in Israel for twenty of those years, David grew up without ever seeing what it looked like to honor the presence of God. It had been written about, but no one had ever demonstrated it. So in his haste and excitement he thought, "Let me just go get it." I imagine he thought there would be some people, perhaps the priests and Levites, who would know what to do with it.

In the midst of our perfectly timed services God is inviting us to a new place. The question is, Who wants to go?

The troops set the ark on a new cart, and Abinadab's sons, Uzzah and Ahio, guided the cart. Since they were priests after their father, everyone must have thought they knew how the ark of God's presence was to be carried. But it turned out that this was not the way, and as creation recognizes the holiness, power, majesty, and presence of the Creator (Rom. 8:19–21), the oxen that carried the ark stumbled. I believe they instinctually knew the people were not handling God's presence with awe and reverence. I believe they sensed that was not how God's presence was supposed to be moved. I believe they sensed that He was supposed to be handled better than that. So they stumbled as if to say, "Not on my watch will you dishonor the Creator."

To keep the ark from falling, Uzzah stuck out his hand to correct what creation was trying to correct. He put his hands on the glory, trying to control how God would move, as if to say, "No, God doesn't go this way. It's supposed to go this way." But at the time of Moses and Aaron, God had given specific instruction that holy things such as the ark were not to be touched by undesignated people: "They must not touch the sacred objects, or they will die" (Num. 4:15).

There is another important element to this that I need to point out here. If you go back to 1 Samuel 6, you'll find that the Philistines were anxious to return the ark after seven months of suffering curses because of their wrongful possession of it. They were never supposed to be in possession of the presence of God. But I want to point out that they also moved the ark by cart. They—who did not know, who were uncircumcised and outside of the covenant, and who were symbolic of the world—had a way they thought God should have been moved. They put Him on a cart because they didn't know any better.

But the people of God knew better. As people of covenant, they were the ones who had an encounter with God. They had a history with Him. There should have been no way they would have done the same thing as the Philistines. They tried to move the presence of God using the same methodology as the world, but there is a way God is to be honored.

> *Things are happening in the earth right now. God is removing people who have caused the body of Christ to believe that our holy God is common. He is not common; He is holy.*

Going back, the Bible says the anger of the Lord was kindled against Uzzah, and he died there in the presence of God. Why? Because of his irreverence, because he didn't fear the Lord, and because there is a way to honor the presence of God. If seventy people died for looking into the ark (1 Sam. 6:19),[1] the Philistines got tumorous boils for being around it (1 Sam. 5:6), and the Philistines' god Dagon was broken down in his temple because he was next to the ark (1 Sam. 5:2–4), what would make Uzzah, knowing that history, think he could touch it?

He touched it because to him it wasn't the presence; it was a relic. It represented old traditions, past moves, and things God wasn't doing anymore. Perhaps he touched it while it was in his father's house, and nothing happened to him. The difference in this instance was that God was not about to be publicly dishonored in a way that caused the people to see a holy God as common.

Things are happening in the earth right now. God is removing people who have caused the body of Christ to believe that our holy

God is common. He is not common; He is holy. And those who think otherwise are being exposed. There is a way to honor the presence of God.

- -

Stories
of the River

If you've ever known anyone personally who has been diagnosed with and lives with lupus, then you are very much aware of how painful and debilitating that sickness can be. There is no medical cure for it, but that didn't stop Ana from coming up front one day, believing that God would heal her.

We've never had a "healing service" at our church, but we have seen over two hundred miracles take place in the presence of God. When the Healer is in the room, healing happens. Ana, who is a woman of faith, knows this to be true, so she didn't hesitate to ask God for her healing and agree in faith when we prayed.

Ana felt the power of God when we prayed and was convinced that she was healed. Walking in that faith, she went back to the doctor and was tested for lupus again. After receiving the test results, she came back to church with a yellow folder. On one side were her former tests showing the diagnosis of lupus, and on the other side was the medical documentation that she was free of lupus.

Jesus healed Ana, but she wasn't going to let the moment go by without asking for total healing. Every year for ten years she had tested positive for precancerous cells in her body. When she was tested again after she received prayer, no precancerous cells were found. Ana was healed of lupus and the precancerous cells in her body. It's happening!

- -

WORTHY HOSTS

The day Uzzah died was the day all of Israel feared the Lord, including King David. King David didn't know there was a way to carry the presence of God. He grew up in a generation that was around the things of God but not intimately acquainted with God. That's what I'm afraid of in this generation. We know the worship songs, we know the lingo, and we have the lights, the smoke, and the screens. We have everything but God Himself, it seems sometimes. We have everything but people who actually know how to get to God Himself and honor Him the way He deserves.

Instead of pushing past the shocking event of Uzzah dying on the spot, David decided not to move the ark to the City of David as he planned. He decided to take it to the house of Obed-edom while he learned God's requirements (2 Sam. 6:10). At Obed-edom's house something interesting happens. The Bible says, "The Ark of the LORD remained there in Obed-edom's house for three months, and the LORD blessed Obed-edom and his entire household" (2 Sam. 6:11).

Who was Obed-edom? He had not been mentioned before now as a set-apart priest or Levite. There doesn't seem to be anything significant about the man himself. Yet the Bible says everything surrounding Obed-edom was blessed. That's amazing. Understand that it wasn't the ark being in his house that caused the blessing. The ark had been in Abinadab's house for twenty years, and there was no mention of a blessing. Three months at Obed-edom's house, and everything was blessed. It wasn't the ark; it was the host.

Notice that there wasn't anything that Obed-edom did to be the chosen host of the presence, but there were things he did to keep it. During the time that our church has been seeing tangible evidence of the presence of God in our midst, there was a moment in one of our rivers (services) when God literally walked into the room. He asserted His sovereign will and decided that our church was to be a habitation for His presence.

I'll never forget this moment as long as I live. I was out of town with my team leading a night of worship. It was a ticketed event, and the room was full. They introduced us, and we went onto the stage and began to lead the people in songs of worship. We were on our third song when I began to feel a really intense heat on my neck and back. It was so hot that I kept turning around and looking up to see if maybe I was standing near a light or some kind of heat source. If you've ever been under the lights on a stage, you know they can get quite hot. I was thinking perhaps I was under one or close to one, but I kept looking, and there was nothing there.

My good friend Clay, who has co-produced all my worship recordings with me, was on the keyboard that night, and he saw me looking around and asked what was wrong. I told him I felt a warm heat on my neck and back. He gave me a quizzical look, but we were in the middle of a song, so I closed my eyes. Immediately I recognized the presence of the Lord right beside me. He was the source of the heat. I had heard of that phenomenon before but never experienced it myself. The significant manifestations of healing had just begun at our church, and I sensed that the power of the Lord was present to heal in that moment. So I began to share about the roughly thirty miracles we had experienced at that time. The word of our testimonies builds faith for the future, so I knew that in telling what God had been doing, faith was being stirred in the room.

As I began to flow this direction, the heat continued on my neck and back, and I sensed that the Lord wanted to heal people in the room with neck and back issues. Remember that it was a ticketed concert at a church in Boston, so I wasn't at my home church and didn't have a relationship with that particular church. Therefore, I asked for permission to continue flowing that direction. I was initially told yes, so I called for people who were dealing with neck and back issues to come forward. Several people came to the front where I was standing. As I prepared to pray for the people, I was passed a note. The note said, "I'm sorry, but you are not permitted to pray for these people because Bishop isn't here."

The moment I read the note, instantly the heat left! I had never felt anything like what I felt in that moment. I've been pursuing God all my life and have become sensitive to His presence, and I had never in my life felt the Lord withdraw. He had come to be with His people, but when I read the note, it was as if He was rejected. I was so grieved by what I felt that I could not continue. It was a ticketed event, but I sang one more song and left the stage. I thought, "If He's not here, why am I here? Apart from Him we can do nothing." I went back to my hotel room and wept like a baby. I kept saying, "God, whatever You wanted to do there please do here [referring to our church in Orlando]." I just kept saying that over and over and over: "Whatever You wanted to do there please do here!" I kept telling Him, "We won't reject You."

I flew home that Saturday, and I kept praying the same thing over and over. I couldn't get over what I felt. Interestingly enough, I received an email saying the two people who were standing closest to me when I felt that heat were healed of their back issues, even though I didn't pray for anyone. That's amazing, but I knew there was more. As I studied and spent time with God all day Saturday, I continued to cry, "Whatever You wanted to do there please do here because we won't reject You."

The next morning, which was Sunday, I woke up praying the same prayer, and while I was driving to church, I felt the heat again. It was as if the Lord got into the car with me to say, "I'll be there." In fact, as I am writing this, I feel His presence the same way. As the service began, I had an expectation of having an encounter. I didn't know when, but I expected Him to answer my prayer. I stood up to preach, and it happened! Once again the presence of the Lord manifested in a way that everyone was aware, and no one could do anything but lie prostrate before God and weep. I was attempting to preach a message titled "The Second Invitation," and those who have heard it say you can literally hear the moment when God walked into the room. The musicians have told me they weren't playing the sounds you can hear on this recording.

Then there was the heat that from that time to now has been one of the evidences to me that the power of the Lord is present. I remember trying to explain it, and people thought they understood until they came near me. Oftentimes when it's happening, others standing around can feel it too. I can't fully explain it, other than to say it's real. That particular day while it was happening, I went to go pray for someone, and all those between me and the person I was praying for experienced the phenomenon of being "slain in the Spirit" when I walked by them, and I never even prayed for them. Obviously it is not me but the presence of the Lord. When it is happening, I remind people that it's not as if I can make heat radiate from my body on command. This is a supernatural thing.

Since that moment our entire household has been blessed. That day can be considered a turning point for us because it was the moment we corporately embraced the idea that we won't reject Him. As a result, He has done more and more. It's amazing what you will experience when you embrace Him instead of rejecting Him. We can't say enough about what God is doing. As I have already mentioned, He healed a whole family from a condition that has never been healed in the history of the United States. He healed a baby who was partially brain-dead. Walkers, canes, and crutches are piling up on our altar because people just don't need them anymore. Various cancers and tumors have been healed and removed. The effects of strokes have been reversed. Paralysis has been reversed. Blind eyes and deaf ears have been opened. Even I was healed of gout, which was debilitating. I can't tell you when it happened because we've been so concentrated on His presence. The only reason I know I've been healed is because I forgot to take my medicine one day, and I just wasn't in pain anymore. I went back to the doctor and was taken off all the medications that had been prescribed for the condition, and I haven't needed them since.

He is healing us because healing comes along with His presence. He says, "I am the LORD who heals you" (Exod. 15:26). We have set Him as our number one affection and pursuit. He is answering our cry. He is all we want. He is all we need. We are not in this moment because we want Him to answer something. We are here because we want Him. And there is nothing we want to do to jeopardize this visitation. We want to continue to have His blessing upon our lives. We want to continue to be hosts for His presence. But are we willing to become more undignified? Are we willing to avoid places that offend Him? Are we willing to make adjustments to the relationships we have to avoid offending Him? Are we willing to stop doing things that offend Him? This is not about our righteousness. This is about our desire to be a host.

There should be nothing we aren't willing to do to make God feel like an honored guest. We shouldn't want anything in our lives to repel Him.

As I travel around this world, I see arks gathering dust in church corners. I go to places where God wants so badly to show up but His presence has been reduced to a monument of the past—a relic. It would seem nobody actually wants to honor Him, because every time He starts to move in a place, we shut it down. We say it's time to move on, time to go, that we have this or that to do. He's asking, "May I have this moment? OK, OK, I'll wait. Oh, I want to heal this person. May I...? OK, I'll wait." He wants to free people who are bound in our churches, but we keep saying, "Not yet." He wants to heal people, and we say, "Sorry, God. Maybe next time. It's 2:00 p.m., and we have to go. We can't hold the people in church too long."

We are in days of visitation, and I'm wondering if there are any people who will host God's presence and give Him the honor He deserves. The ark is moving, and it is seeking to rest in houses that are like Obed-edom's. The question is, Who will host Him?

DAY AFTER DAY AND NIGHT AFTER NIGHT

Earlier in this chapter I introduced the verse in Revelation 4 that shows us the kind of honor God is used to. It says that day after day and night after night heavenly beings worship Him. We keep thinking we're worshipping for a long time because we go for an hour. No! Day after day and night after night they worship in heaven. We keep thinking that just because we have our hands lifted, they get tired, we pull them down, and maybe we cry a few tears, that is enough. No, that's not enough. Day after day and night after night. What do we think Obed-edom was doing in order to receive the blessing of God's presence? He was giving God what He is used to— worship day after day, night after night.

The ark of the covenant is moving and wants a place to dwell. Will you be a worthy host? Will you give God the atmosphere of worship He is used to? What will be your posture before Him? Will you treat Him as they did in Abinadab's house? Will you put Him in a corner?

The Bible says in 2 Samuel 6:12, "Then King David was told, 'The LORD has blessed Obed-edom's household and everything he has because of the Ark of God.' So David went there and brought the Ark of God from the house of Obed-edom to the City of David with a great celebration." David and the people of Israel figured out right way to carry the ark. So they hadn't moved more than six steps before "David sacrificed a bull and a fattened calf" (2 Sam. 6:13). Further study into this scripture reveals that they did not stop just this one time on the way to Jerusalem. They stopped every six steps.[2] There was a continual worship. They gave God what He is used to. They stopped to show their gratitude, worship, and honor.

The Bible says there was great fanfare. They had all sorts of music and singing and dancing because they were so excited that they would no longer be a generation that would try to operate apart from the presence of God.

Verse 20 tells of King David dancing out of his robe. He and all the people were so excited that God would be near to them.

> They brought in the ark of God and placed it inside the tent which David had pitched for it, and they offered burnt offerings and peace offerings before God. When David had finished offering the burnt offering and the peace offerings, he blessed the people in the name of the LORD. He distributed to everyone of Israel, both man and woman, to everyone a loaf of bread and a portion of meat and a raisin cake.
>
> He appointed some of the Levites as ministers before the ark of the LORD, even to celebrate and to thank and praise the LORD God of Israel: Asaph the chief, and second to him Zechariah, then Jeiel, Shemiramoth, Jehiel, Mattithiah, Eliab, Benaiah, Obed-edom and Jeiel, with

musical instruments, harps, lyres; also Asaph played loud-
sounding cymbals, and Benaiah and Jahaziel the priests
blew trumpets continually before the ark of the covenant
of God.

—1 CHRONICLES 16:1–6, NASB

Look who was in the group of Levites—Obed-edom. He did not
live in Jerusalem, but he got in on honoring God since His presence
had been at his house and since he had had an encounter with Him.
He adjusted his life all over again, risking it all to be one of the hosts
of the presence of God. He could not go back to life as usual.

Then verses 37–38 of 1 Chronicles 16 blessed me. They say, "So
he left Asaph and his relatives there before the ark of the covenant
of the LORD to minister before the ark continually, as every day's
work required; and Obed-edom with his 68 relatives" (NASB). What
have we discovered God is used to? Praise, worship, and honor day
after day and night after night. Can I tell you a secret? I keep worship music playing in our church every single day, twenty-four hours
a day. Until we can have the kind of house where we have Asaph-
type people who minister to him continually, we're at least going to
keep an atmosphere.

It may seem as if it's too much—day after day and night after
night, worshipping and spending time with God. But it is all worth
it. The encounter with God that you are having even now as you
read this book is going to affect your entire family. When Obed-
edom decided he was going to leave his hometown and go after God,
sixty-eight of his family members went after God too. It's OK to
stay in the presence of God, because your family is coming with you.

EVEN MORE UNDIGNIFIED

But before your family joins you, you may have to deal with these
questions: "Why have you been at church so long? What have you
been doing there? I just don't get it. I don't understand." This happened to David when he returned home after repossessing the ark
of God. Second Samuel 6:20 says: "When David returned home

to bless his own family, Michal, the daughter of Saul, came out to meet him. She said in disgust, 'How distinguished the king of Israel looked today, shamelessly exposing himself to the servant girls like any vulgar person might do!'"

What was Michal doing? She was looking at him out of her window. Sometimes when you have an encounter with God, the people who once helped you and stood by you will question and criticize you. Earlier in Scripture (1 Sam. 19:12) Michal helped David escape through a window when Saul was trying to kill him. But now that he had an encounter with God, she said she was disgusted—and maybe she was jealous because she had not had such an experience.

His response was bold: "I was dancing before the LORD, who chose me above your father and all his family! He appointed me as the leader of Israel, the people of the LORD, so I celebrate before the LORD. Yes, and I am willing to look even more foolish than this, even to be humiliated in my own eyes!" (2 Sam. 6:21–22). I like the way the New King James Version of the Bible puts it: "And I will be even more undignified than this."

Some of us have been holding back our praise and adoration of God. We don't know that it's OK to become undignified in the presence of God and really worship like David because it has never been demonstrated to us before. David had no one to show him how to host the presence of God, but he was patient. He waited on the Lord, and God began to teach him by His Spirit. And old and ancient pathways began to surface.

What David discovered is that it is OK to go crazy before God. It's OK to lose your mind before God. It's OK for you to make a sacrifice of praise and worship every six steps. It's OK for you to stomp, dance, leap, and cry out. It's OK. You're not crazy. This is what God is used to. You are giving Him what He is worthy of. You're not crazy; He's just worthy. You're not crazy; He's that good! You're not crazy; He's that amazing. You're not crazy; He's that holy. Don't hold back. Give Him what He's used to—day after day and night after night.

Do you know why I've decided I don't want to control anything? Because where He moves I move. Where He goes I go. I do not want to be one of the ones who say, "Do you remember those days of visitation?" I am like Obed-edom: whenever David comes to get the ark, I'm going with him.

Let those who don't have the revelation that it's happening keep talking about you. They're coming. Let them continue to make fun of you. They're coming! Let them keep resisting. They're coming! Because when God blesses you and you are a worthy host of His presence, your whole family, your neighbors, and your coworkers will see it. And they are going to say, "I want that too!"

RESPOND

God is here. Revival is happening. We are encountering the Lord, and we can't go back to normal. His presence changes everything— our behavior, where we go, what we say, and who we want to be around. Don't apologize for it. Some may believe you think you are too good. But it's not that; it's that you'll do whatever you have to do to stay with Him because you are a host of His presence. Yes, it's that serious for you now. He is more valuable to you than anybody and anything else.

We're talking about a life-changing, life-altering encounter with the presence of God. Once you've experienced it, what is there to go back to?

CHAPTER 11

HE IS HERE—NOW WHAT WILL YOU DO?

Ask the LORD for rain in the spring, for he makes the storm clouds. And he will send showers of rain so every field becomes a lush pasture.

—ZECHARIAH 10:1

Ask the LORD for rain in the time of the latter rain. The LORD will make flashing clouds; He will give them showers of rain, grass in the field for everyone.

—ZECHARIAH 10:1, NKJV

WHEN IT COMES to recognizing the movement of God, most of us want things to be crystal clear. We would love to have God wave a big red flag at us and say, "This is Me! Here I am. It's really Me moving." But when it comes to the things of God, many times He won't use big signs to get our attention. He will use subtle things, and most of us pass them by, thereby missing windows of opportunity. We fail the test of subtlety and miss divine moments.

There are certain moments in time and seasons in the Spirit that present themselves as windows of opportunity. Zechariah 10:1 puts us right in the midst of one such moment. It's raining, and most people don't pray for rain when it's raining. We pray for rain in seasons of drought. But this verse is directing us to do something different: Don't wait until there's a drought to ask for rain. Ask for rain in the time of rain. This is going to be important for us to understand in terms of sustaining the move of God. What the verse implies is that we need to use the open window of opportunity (an open heaven pouring down rain) to seize the moment to ask for more.

Now you must understand how we can miss a moment. A moment is a very short period of time, or a particular time, or a precise point in time. So it's not hard to see how it could pass us by. This is why we must become aware of what God is doing so that when a moment of opportunity presents itself, we can seize it.

CREATE A WINDOW

Now this is important. Seizing a moment creates momentum, and momentum is a strength or force something has when it's moving. It's a strength or force that causes something to get stronger or faster as time passes. Momentum works in such a way that it takes more effort to get something moving than to keep it moving. We are aware that what we have stepped into at Deeper is a season that took years of intercession to see and that will take ongoing intercession to maintain.

Intercession creates a window.

During one of our monthly Presence Nights, I remember a man of God joining us for worship. He didn't need to identify himself; I knew who he was. I knew he was a pastor and was a prophetic voice. I knew he had been in the Orlando area for a long time. But he didn't ask for any preferential treatment. He didn't make an announcement, "I'm coming. I want a special seat. Do you know who I am?" He just came and worshipped and wept.

Don't wait until there's a drought to ask for rain. Ask for rain in the time of rain.

At the very end of the service, I went to greet him, and he just began to release a number of things the Lord had shown him. He was weeping as he said to me, "I prayed for years to see this." What we have been seeing in our church he was not seeing in his, even though he spent his life interceding for what we are now experiencing in our city. He was weeping tears of joy because even though it wasn't happening specifically at his church with a group of people he was leading, he was seeing the fruit of his intercession beginning to break out and manifest somewhere. We reject the idea that we reached the place we are in on our own. It took people who laid down their lives to see a move of God in this region.

We don't often know the price intercessors will pay to see a move of God happen in a particular region. Back in the 1980s I knew of an intercessor who spent her retirement savings to travel to all fifty states so she could pray on the steps of all fifty state capitols. Nameless and faceless people such as this woman have laid down their lives so other people could step into an open heaven. They lay down their lives to create a window for other people to seize the moment.

Revival doesn't just show up. I don't ever want our church to take it for granted and feel as if we prayed and this happened. No. We joined intercession that was already taking place. We stand on the shoulders of nameless and faceless people whom we've never met and who walked this city and died having never seen what they had been praying for come to pass. We must be careful not to take things for granted because we didn't pay for them.

Years of intercession led to a moment. Continued intercession leads to momentum.

- -

Stories
of the River

Rebecca and her son had been attending our church for a while. Her son was deaf in one ear, but like many resilient people, they didn't allow that to stop them from living a normal life. As they encountered obstacles, they faced them with a smile.

One of the most amazing things about this outpouring is that oftentimes people get healed without even specifically asking just because Jesus the

Healer is near. That's what happened to Rebecca's
son. One day during the service he was healed. No
one prayed for him. He just suddenly was able to
hear. The healing was so low-key. He didn't even
alert his mom right away. On the car ride home
he casually said, "Mom, I can hear you." She said,
"That's great, baby." He said, "No, Mom, I can hear
you!" Now realizing what he was really saying, Rebecca began to praise God. Her son was healed.
He was no longer deaf in one ear. His hearing was
completely restored, and no one but God could
possibly take the credit or the glory because no
one had a hand in it but God. It's happening!

STIFLE THE MOMENT

Revival requires continual movement—momentum. Momentum
requires an environment where movement is unimpeded, where
nothing is blocking forward progress. That's why Paul wrote in 1
Thessalonians 5:19, "Do not stifle [or quench] the Holy Spirit." In
other words, don't stop your spiritual momentum, because once you
stop momentum, it takes more effort than you needed when you
started to get it going again. In the case of revival, that is a costly
stoppage that takes a lifetime to see again.

Don't stifle the moment. Don't quench the Holy Spirit.

I remember as a child—and we joke about this stuff now—going
to my grandmother's church in the morning and, while church was
going on, smelling food. After service we would go to the fellowship hall, eat the food, and then return to the sanctuary for another
service. We never left! Many of us look back at this now and think,
"No way!"

Not too long ago I was in Nigeria for a night of worship. It was
held outdoors in an open field with about fifteen thousand to twenty
thousand people in attendance. The night started at 6:00 p.m., but
we didn't get on the platform until 1:00 a.m., and the last guest went
up at 3:00 a.m. There were no chairs to sit down on, yet nobody left.
In Western churches if pastors preach for more than forty minutes,

we start getting antsy. We have places to go, people to see, and things to do. I ask this next question sincerely, and I think all of us need to honestly assess our answers: What place, person, or thing has more importance than God?

We have boiled down the Scripture and the presence of God in our corporate gatherings to less than an hour per week, in some cases, expecting God is going to move. In Acts 20 the Bible talks about Paul preaching so long that a young man fell asleep on a windowsill, fell out the window, and died. Instead of ending the service, Paul went down, raised the boy from the dead, and kept preaching. So we're at this point now where some of our churches are seeing miracles happen in our midst. We see God heal people. We see God deliver people. We see God set people free. We are excited—it's cool—but we still have this tendency to not make God's presence preeminent, where we still want to be out of church by a certain time.

Years of intercession led to a moment. Continued intercession leads to momentum.

In traveling to places such as the continent of Africa and witnessing thousands of people gathering in worship for nine or ten hours at a time or in hearing about the revivals and awakenings in South and Central America, I am moved to pray for the church of America. The only thing is the church of America is violating 1 Thessalonians 5:19. We do quench the Holy Spirit. He starts to move, and we act as if we are uncomfortable with it. I should probably take the surprise out of it: the move of God will make people uncomfortable. Guests will be uncomfortable. Unbelievers will be uncomfortable. How do you expect an unbeliever to be saved except that the Holy Spirit reveals Jesus?

Any man who can be convinced into accepting something can also be convinced out of it. Our job is not to convince people that Jesus is a good idea. The Holy Spirit reveals to them that He's the only way. Jesus is not explained; He's revealed. How can the Spirit reveal Him if the Spirit is being stifled by our programs or our discomfort with the way He moves? If you have had a true encounter with God, it's because Jesus Himself was revealed by the Spirit in the midst of His free-flowing presence.

When it comes down to it, people are not interested in our trying to preach as if we're doing a TED Talk. Preaching devoid of power and preaching devoid of signs and wonders will not change a life. It may change a mind, but it won't change a life. We must allow the Spirit of God to flow freely.

The Time to Ask for More Is Now

As we are in a moment of revival, the time to ask for more is now. Unfortunately during this spiritual spring season, some people are saying not to do this and not to do that. "Don't worship this long." "Don't preach this long." "Don't keep people this long." "Don't call for 5:00 a.m. prayer." "Don't call for 7:00 a.m. prayer." "Don't ask them to come to church more often." As a result, we have an entire generation that is not experiencing the things of God and is squandering the intercession that came before us.

Jesus is not explained; He's revealed.

How is it that we are now a culture that doesn't value the revival moments for which people laid down their lives in prayer and never saw? How is it that we are a church culture that doesn't want to come to church and doesn't want to stay? Revival is for the believer first, for a church that has fallen asleep. Revival is for something that was once alive but now is dead—something that was once moving but now is stagnant. In truth, revival is needed because the church has fallen asleep. Revival in the church causes a reformation in the world.

That is why if there is ever an outpour of the rains of revival anywhere in the world, we need to be asking for more rain. We need to ask for the rain during the time of rain. It is costly to miss the moment and realize how dry we are once the rain has stopped. We may find ourselves waiting awhile for the rain to fall again—possibly waiting for generation after generation. We can't afford the cost. We can't miss the moment.

QUIET THE NOISE; RELEASE A SOUND

Divine moments can be created. The moment of time we're in right now—both our church and the body of Christ—was created. A divine moment is an intersection where heaven meets earth. We create this intersection when we align with the things of heaven, and we can create divine moments with a sound. Let me show you what I mean.

Mark 10:46–52 says:

> Then they reached Jericho, and as Jesus and his disciples left town, a large crowd followed him. A blind beggar named Bartimaeus (son of Timaeus) was sitting beside the road. When Bartimaeus heard that Jesus of Nazareth was nearby, he began to shout, "Jesus, Son of David, have mercy on me!"
>
> "Be quiet!" many of the people yelled at him.
>
> But he only shouted louder, "Son of David, have mercy on me!"
>
> When Jesus heard him, he stopped and said, "Tell him to come here."
>
> So they called the blind man. "Cheer up," they said. "Come on, he's calling you!" Bartimaeus threw aside his coat, jumped up, and came to Jesus.
>
> "What do you want me to do for you?" Jesus asked.
>
> "My Rabbi," the blind man said, "I want to see!"
>
> And Jesus said to him, "Go, for your faith has healed you." Instantly the man could see, and he followed Jesus down the road.

In chapter 9 we looked at the story of the woman with the issue of blood. Well, once again we find Jesus in a similar setting—surrounded by a large crowd. Bartimaeus, who was blind but had other heightened senses, knew that the atmosphere of his city had changed. The buzz and the noise of the crowd might have led him to ask, "What's going on? Why are all these people here? Why is there suddenly a buzz?" And maybe someone answered, "Jesus is here."

Now imagine what went on inside his heart when he heard that response: "Jesus is here." Everything he had ever heard about Him up to that moment probably came rushing to his mind: the deliverances of the man with the unclean spirit, the demoniac in the garden, the demoniac boy, and the Syrophoenician woman's daughter; the healings of Simon's mother-in-law, the leper, the man with the withered hand, Jairus's daughter, the afflicted woman, the deaf and the dumb man, and the blind man near Bethsaida; the stilling of the storm and Jesus's walking on water; the feedings of the four thousand and the five thousand; and so many more.

As we are in a moment of revival in the earth, the time to ask for more is now.

Can you imagine it? He had heard about Jesus before Jesus reached him, so he might have been thinking, "All this has happened, and now the man who is responsible for it all is near me?" The crowd got closer. He could hear them passing by. He knew a once-in-a-lifetime moment was upon him. The Bible says he lifted up his voice and said, "Jesus, Son of David, have mercy on me!" He was determined to not let this moment pass him by. He was going to ask for rain in the time of rain. He was asking for a moment while the moment was there. He was going to seize that moment.

We tend to read his cry—"Jesus, Son of David, have mercy on me"—as if the environment were relatively calm and quiet, but it was not calm or quiet at all. He was in the midst of a large crowd. If he was using a calm and quiet tone, the only people who would have heard him were those in close proximity to him. Have you ever tried to get the attention of someone in a noisy place? Have you ever been in an arena and seen a friend and found yourself screaming and looking crazy trying to get his attention? This is what Bartimaeus was doing. And even with all the noise he was making, Bartimaeus could not move the crowd. Many of them probably didn't even hear him.

Can I turn the narrative on its head for a moment? There's a difference between a noise and a sound.

The people were yelling at Bartimaeus and telling him to be quiet. They wanted him to stop making a scene. But desperation ignores detractors and distractions, so he kept crying out. And in the middle of a large, noisy crowd, Jesus stopped. I need you to get this. There were thousands of people asking Jesus for something or trying in some way to get His attention. They weren't walking along in silence. And somehow through the thousands of people who were walking, something got Jesus's attention. The Bible says He heard Bartimaeus and stopped. There's a difference between making noise and releasing a sound.

Noise surrounded Jesus, but a sound stopped Him. Worry doesn't have a sound, but it makes noise. Fear doesn't have a sound, but it's noisy. Complaining doesn't have a sound; it's just noisy. Doubt doesn't have a sound; it's noisy.

That's why you can get stirred in your emotions, get stressed out, and maybe even shout, trying to get the attention of Jesus, but all you are doing is making noise. But there's a difference between making noise and releasing a sound. Noise might get the attention of people, but only a sound causes Jesus to stop. You might get everyone else to say, "O God, please help her," or, "O God, please help him." Everybody else might understand that you're going through something, but that doesn't necessarily mean your commotion will cause Jesus to stop in His tracks.

Desperation has a sound that cuts through noise. Desperation gets God's attention. Jesus said, "Tell him to come here." Then He asked Bartimaeus, "What do you want Me to do for you?" Don't just make a noise. Release a sound.

WHEN THE MOMENT COMES...

Many people are used to making noise and causing a commotion without carrying any sense of expectancy or faith. So if God does respond—because He is God and can do whatever He wants—they wouldn't know what to say. They wouldn't know how to answer if He were to draw them in and say, "What do you want Me to do for you?" Many believers have learned how to make noise, but they haven't learned to release a sound or what to do if God responds. They open the window but don't know how to keep it open. They end up living in the moment instead of living in momentum.

> *So many people get Jesus's attention but don't know what to do when He comes.*

Be present.

Years ago as a young worship leader, I received an amazing piece of advice. It was actually a rebuke from a pastor, but it was life-changing. He said, "You need to learn how to be present to the moment." It's simple, but that gentle rebuke completely changed the way I lead worship. It completely changed my walk with God, and it will change yours.

Be present to the moment. I wrestled with it for a while. I thought, "What does that even mean?" Then God began to break it down to me. You see, I grew up in a church that had a moment but didn't know how to sustain momentum. Sadly the window closed. To this day there are still people there hoping the window will open again, but they don't understand that they missed the moment. They haven't learned what the sound is, so they don't understand that they can shift from making noise to releasing a sound if they desire to create another divine moment.

Know that you can't re-create it.

It's grieves me to look back at that time when I was a young person growing up in a moment when the window was open and something was happening. It was springtime. Songs were written. Records were recorded. Books were penned. Pastors were released. Then the sound changed to noise, though most people didn't recognize the shift. For a while the noise was still attracting people because of the reputation of the sound. But Jesus wasn't stopping. He kept walking to the next city.

Even I, being young, knew there was a difference, but my immaturity led me to think we could just continue what we were doing. But what I found myself doing everywhere I went after that point was trying to re-create that past moment in the present. Pastor, worship leader, believer, and anyone who is reading these lines right now, hear me when I say we have developed an unhealthy obsession with the things of the past. All the time, we are unknowingly trying to re-create the past. That window is closed.

We say we need to go back and sing those songs. We need to go back and do what they did. If you do those things without the heart of desperation that was released during that moment, you won't get the same result. Those things were birthed in that moment's present reality of desperation. A sound was released. You can't echo a sound, but you can echo noise.

A sound comes out of you in a present moment. You can't grab ahold of a sound that was released in the past. You can only release a sound from your present reality. What the pastor was really saying was that the moment was good. What happened there was good. It was a move of God, an outpouring, a revival, and a stirring of the Spirit. It was a prophetic moment. But that was then. Where are you now?

Be aware of what God is doing and what season it is.

Though it took some time for me to get it, I came to realize I was completely unaware of what God was doing. I was completely unaware of what season it was. I was trying to pull people back, not in.

Many people are living in this moment, as I was. We get stuck in former moves. People come up to me all the time and say, "We should do this because at my other church…" And I'm thinking, "Well, why did you leave?" It's as if we're trying to capture lightning in a bottle and trying to get the old thing and bring it into the present.

Please don't misunderstand me; I'm not talking about principles here. I'm not talking about foundational biblical principles.

I'm talking about how many of us are like zombies. Our bodies are here, but our spirits are there—stuck. So when we shout, we're not releasing a sound. We're making a noise. We may be joining in with those who are releasing a sound, but we're just making a noise because we're not actually desperate. We don't even know we're not actually where we think we are. Disconnected from the present moment, we can't discern how much we need God.

> *If there was a time or season of consecration when you did something that allowed you to hear God, stay there.*

The prophet Zechariah challenges us on the need to be aware of what season we're in. "Ask for the rain in the time of rain." When we are aware, our asking and our crying out will be in tune with God's heart. When it's raining, we'll know it is the time to ask for more and it is the time God will give it.

Stay there.

There is a corporate revival happening, but that doesn't necessarily mean an individual revival is happening in you. It is possible to be *at* a move but not *in* it. It's called a parade. You're standing there, and you're present, but the movement is happening on the street. Corporate revival is happening around you, but personal revival is not happening in you. Why? Because you thought that if you did it once, that was enough.

Spiritual moments exist to create momentum. Whatever you did to create the moment when heaven intersected earth in your life is what you need to continue to do to keep that moment going. Consecration is not an event. It's an alteration of lifestyle.

If there was a time or season of consecration when you did something that allowed you to hear God, stay there. If not watching TV is what caused you to hear God, then keep the TV off. Perpetually. Forever. We may not want to hear stuff like this because we want God on our terms. We want our encounters with Him to work a certain way. We want it done our way. "Come on our terms, God," we say. "Come in our time." And we stifle the Holy Spirit. We say, "OK, that was cool, God. We're good now."

There is no sense of desperation in that kind of response. That response will not cause God to stop in the midst of a multitude and ask, "What is it you want Me to do for you?" But if there is anyone within a generation who will release a sound, Jesus will hear it and stop.

RESPOND

I don't believe it was the audible sound of Bartimaeus's voice that arrested Jesus's attention. Remember when Jesus was on His way to raise Jairus's daughter from the dead? The Bible says that a woman who had been dealing with a blood-flow issue for twelve years touched the hem of His garment. He said, "Who touched Me?" But did He actually feel her hand on His garment? No. He noticed that somebody touched Him differently. Not only did the woman pull on His garment; she also pulled on His life.

May I suggest to you that He might not have felt the garment pull, but He felt the virtue pull? May I suggest to you that He didn't hear Bartimaeus's voice; He heard the sound of desperation?

Some of us keep thinking that if we just get loud enough, if we get demonstrative enough, we'll get Jesus to respond. Let me dissuade you from that line of thinking because you'll end up making noise, and I am here to encourage you to make a sound. Let's step outside of the natural realm for a minute and hear what God is trying to say to us.

Sometimes when we're desperate, a sound can't even come out. Sometimes when we're desperate, it's not our voices that make the sounds; it's our tears. Sometimes when we're desperate, it's not how loud we get; it's how low we bow. Sometimes when we're desperate, it's not how loud we shout; it's how often we sit in silence. Sometimes when we're desperate, we release a sound when we open up the Word and say, "God, I need to hear from You. God, I need You."

Are you perpetually desperate?

Desperation is a sound that your life makes. Desperation is the thing that makes you get up at one, two, or three o'clock in the morning when you're restless, and you start walking your floor and praying. Desperation has nothing to do with how loud you scream. It has everything to do with the sound that your life makes.

Sometimes when we're desperate, it's not our voices that make the sounds; it's our tears.

I encourage you to find your way to a place of desperation and release a sound from there. When you do, you will create a divine moment that will lead to momentum. The moment is here. Jesus has heard and has stopped. What will you do now?

CHAPTER 12

FEED THE FIRE

The fire on the altar must be kept burning; it must
never go out. Each morning the priest will add fresh
wood to the fire and arrange the burnt offering on
it. He will then burn the fat of the peace offerings
on it. Remember, the fire must be kept burning
on the altar at all times. It must never go out.

—LEVITICUS 6:12-13

SOME TIME AGO I had a chance to go to Zimbabwe. It was a
return trip. I'd been to the continent of Africa before. I love
it, and I love the people. But this trip was special. It con-
tained a moment I'll remember forever.

We had been ministering in the area for a few days, and toward the
end of our trip we were invited to the host pastor's home for conversation and refreshment. Upon our arrival we were led out to the patio,
where a seating area had been set up around a blazing fire pit. There
were different things to eat and drink, even marshmallows for roasting.

Normally I am not an outdoorsman, and being outside in the
elements is not my idea of fun. But there was something significant
about being in this moment with this pastor and his family, who had
been in the country for more than thirty-five years. Instead of traditional campfire stories, they shared with us stories of great faith and
their efforts in building a church that had literally changed the nation.

I was stirred as he told us about how being twice removed from
the impartation of John G. Lake had impacted the effectiveness of
their ministry over the years. I was so enthralled by their testimony,
my spirit being fed, that I must have forgotten we were outside. You
know how there are just some moments that are so precious you

don't want to do anything to disturb them, so you will do whatever it takes to keep them? This was one of those moments.

Until…

Out of the corner of my eye I saw something move in the darkness away from the light of the fire. It looked like a dog, but it was a rat—a cane rat. We don't have those in the United States, and for the Americans reading this book, you ought to thank God. Not even the New York City subway rats can compare to these giant things. A cane rat could eat a subway rat, it's so big.

So for about two to three minutes there was mass pandemonium among the group. We screamed and shooed, stomped and shouted, each of us doing whatever we could to get away from the rat. Then the pastor yelled, "Don't let that thing in the house," and everybody started chasing it and trying to scare it away. In confusion and terror, of course, the rat started coming toward me. I took off. One of my pastors, who had taken the trip with me, said he had never seen me move so fast. Listen, I don't do outside.

Things settled down, and I apprehensively rejoined the group and discovered that they didn't kill the rat; they just chased it into the woods next to the fire. But somehow we all felt peace enough to sit back down. Someone threw more wood on the fire, and the conversation continued.

The fellowship we shared must have been a move of God. Had it been any other time, my normal MO would have led me to say, "This meeting, this time of being out in front of a fire in Africa, is over. I'm good. Take me back to the hotel." But no. God was present. It was one of those moments so precious you don't want to disturb it, so you will do whatever it takes to make it last. So we sat there knowing that a rat the size of a dog lurked in the nearby woods but that we would be OK as long as we kept the fire burning.

FUELING A FIRE FOR THE FUTURE

As they talked about how God had been moving in the nation of Zimbabwe since they planted their church, their stories and testimonies resonated deeply within me. The family imparted to us an anointing that was so sweet and so closely linked to what God had been doing at Deeper. As I listened, the Lord spoke to me, saying that there are supposed to be rivers flowing out of our little warehouse church that will affect the nations of the earth.

This is why I cannot help but feel the places the Lord has sent me to are to expose me to a level of faith and vision that challenge what I think is possible. If you position yourself as a student, God will put you in a place where you can see and hear things that seed in you a faith for the future. When you get there, don't try to make everyone understand why you're supposed to be there. It is for you to know and trust that God put you there. As He has done for me, God will allow you to be around people and circumstances that will ignite your faith and expectation, causing you to become uncomfortable with where you are. When it's time to turn up the heat on what He wants to do, God will put you with people who move in the Spirit in a way that provokes righteous envy. You will want what they have.

If you are like me, then you will understand when I say I am in the most unique and odd season of my life, where I am desperately crying out to be used by God in a significant way. This may seem strange if you know of my ministry as a worship leader. You may even be saying, "You're already being used by God in a significant way." But there's something in me that keeps crying out for more.

Even though the Lord has allowed me to experience a lot of amazing things, I'm nowhere close to being used at the magnitude God has shown me. Most of what I have been walking in during the last decade with music and such I really didn't see. With all that the Lord is doing at Deeper Fellowship, I am just now walking in the "exceedingly abundantly" I had envisioned. At the same time, "far above what you could ask, think, or imagine" is still far ahead of me. (See Ephesians 3:20.) It is an interesting place to be when you can look back over your life and be grateful for the amazing things God has enabled you to experience yet still look ahead and be desperate for more.

As I sit and listen to stories of faith about nations changing and turning to God, there is something in my DNA that says I don't want to just be in attendance when the move of God hits. I want to be part of it. I used to say, "God, I want to see it." Now I am saying, "God, I want to see it here." There is a holy dissatisfaction that keeps me up at night. It causes me to recognize that there is more. I long for it. It burns on the inside of me. Is it burning inside you? If so, let's talk about how to keep it burning.

Stories
of the River

We've experienced many unique moments during this outpouring, but one of the most memorable was in April of 2017 during our monthly Presence Night. We were also celebrating our third anniversary as a church and had a couple of guests with us. Due to the size of our building and the notoriety of some of my friends in ministry, at times we won't say publicly who is coming to be with us. But inevitably word gets out, and more people than usual show up. There is typically a line to get in, and sometimes we have to turn people away due to space restrictions. This particular Presence Night in April was one of those times.

As a pastor it breaks my heart to have to turn away people who come to encounter God. We had a guest speaker that night, but my friend Travis Greene, who also happens to be a Grammy-nominated, multiple award–winning worship leader, was our guest worship leader. We were in the back preparing to go into the service when I received word that we were at full capacity and there were still hundreds of people outside. Travis said he would take his guitar outside and lead worship for the people who couldn't get inside. I thought that was an amazing idea. We've had several services when people have literally stood outside for hours while the service was taking place just to listen through the walls at what was happening inside.

I offered to go out with Travis as he led worship. When we went outside, I noticed a woman to my left who was wearing a neck brace and slumped over with a cane. I thought to myself that she had probably heard of the many miracles that had taken place, so out of sheer compassion I walked over to her to pray for her. I asked her what her issue was, and she said she was dealing with fibromyalgia. I began to pray for her as Travis was leading worship a few feet away from me. What happened next was unexpected. As I was praying for her, I began to hear hissing and a spitting sound. I looked up, and the woman was hissing and spitting like a snake. At that moment my prayer changed, and I went from praying for the woman's healing to rebuking the devil. You can only imagine the scene. Hundreds of people are outside singing, and here I am on the side rebuking an evil spirit.

As I began to command the devil to come out of this lady, she began to scream, "No, she's mine!" Now we have quite a scene. People who had their phones out recording Travis were now recording a demon being cast out of a lady outside the building. After some prayer, not only did the Lord set her free from the demon, but she also was healed of all the symptoms of fibromyalgia. She left without her cane and neck brace and said she had no pain anywhere. It's happening!

- -

KEEP THE FIRE BURNING

Give Aaron and his sons the following instructions regarding the burnt offering. The burnt offering must be left on top of the altar until the next morning, and the fire on the altar must be kept burning all night. In the morning, after the priest on duty has put on his official linen clothing and linen undergarments, he must clean out the ashes of the burnt offering and put them beside the altar. Then he must take off these garments, change back into his regular

clothes, and carry the ashes outside the camp to a place
that is ceremonially clean. Meanwhile, the fire on the altar
must be kept burning; it must never go out. Each morning
the priest will add fresh wood to the fire and arrange the
burnt offering on it. He will then burn the fat of the peace
offerings on it. Remember, the fire must be kept burning
on the altar at all times. It must never go out.

—Leviticus 6:9–13

When we were sitting in front of the fire in Africa, in order to
keep it burning, they didn't add more fire. They added more wood.
As long as it has something to consume, fire will keep burning. The
only time fire dies is when there is nothing for it to feed on.

The Bible says in Hebrews 12:29 that our God is an all-
consuming fire, and the instruction to the Levitical priest in
Leviticus 6 was to not let the fire go out. This was important to
God; He said it twice because He knew the natural proclivity of
man is to take our eyes off what's important and let the fire die.

There's something about this generation—and this is more about
mind-set than age group—that as soon as something is not hot for
us, we want to move on to something else. But God has given us
a responsibility and an assignment, just as He gave the priests in
Leviticus—not to ignite the fire but to not let the fire die. So when
we pray, "God, set me on fire for You," we pray in error. There was a
fire set at the cross that we are responsible for keeping lit. We ought
to be asking God what He wants us to add to the fire so it will burn
without dying out.

Fire dies when it has nothing to consume.

There is a lot at stake with learning how to feed the fire of God.
Every fire has a starting point, what arson investigators call ignition.
In our desire to be part of what God is doing in the earth, we can
increase our effectiveness by remembering what God has done and
how He wants us to respond. The first two ignition points reveal
God's contribution to the fire. The last two reveal ours.

Ignition Point 1: Burnt Offerings

> The LORD called to Moses from the Tabernacle and said to him, "Give the following instructions to the people of Israel. When you present an animal as an offering to the LORD, you may take it from your herd of cattle or your flock of sheep and goats. If the animal you present as a burnt offering is from the herd, it must be a male with no defects. Bring it to the entrance of the Tabernacle so you may be accepted by the LORD. Lay your hand on the animal's head, and the LORD will accept its death in your place to purify you, making you right with him."
>
> —LEVITICUS 1:1–4

This is substitutionary atonement in a nutshell, a foreshadowing of what Christ would ultimately do on our behalf. Romans chapter 3 talks about our being made right with God through our faith in Christ, "and this is true for everyone who believes, no matter who we are" (v. 22). While atoning—making up for—one's sins was literal for the people of Israel in the Old Testament, it is by faith in Christ for us now.

Romans 6:23 says that "the wages of sin is death," but death was too high a price for us to pay before Christ because everything was literal. Everything was done in the natural. You wouldn't get back up if you laid down your own life. But this is what God required; He required life. "Without the shedding of blood," Hebrews 9:22 tells us, "there is no forgiveness" of sin. Blood represents life. Christ shed His blood so we wouldn't have to. He took our place and died, but in the Old Testament, the animal sacrifice represented a person's sin-life. God created a visceral way for them to see what the exchange rate was for their sin-life by instituting the burnt offering as their atonement, as their way for being made right and thereby righteous enough to approach Him.

The reason it was important for the priests to keep the fire going was because as long as their sin-life was dead, they had access to God. If that exchange was ever cut short, if the fire ever went out, their access also would be cut off. Because humankind sins continually, there had to be a continual sacrifice, giving us continual access to the Father. He saw fit, in His desire to stay in communion with His people, that the sacrificial fire remain burning. God wanted to set a constant reminder in heaven and on earth of our access to Him.

In other words, because He is holy and set apart and we broke covenant at the fall of Adam and Eve, and because Christ had not yet come to be our substitutionary atonement once and for all, God instituted something on earth so we could see what the cost of true worship is. The true cost of worship is not a song but our life, which is acceptable because of His life. This is worship many of us now take for granted. We lift our hands if we want. We engage with it if our emotions say we feel like it. But being able to go into the presence of God without fear of our sins instantly condemning us to death is only two thousand years old. For millennia, people offered sacrifices they feared might not be accepted.

Consider this: In the Old Testament if people wanted to go into the house of worship, they couldn't arrive without an animal sacrifice. They would not be accepted into the presence of God if they came the way we come now. And if you think worship is messy when you cry or someone is on the floor, then you would have thought worship was really messy back then. Some of us can't handle seeing our own blood. Imagine dealing with another creature's blood. Imagine the smell and the stench.

Yet to God the burnt offering reminded Him that even though we sin, He still loves us. Even though we've broken covenant, He will accept us back, set us right, and complete the work He began in us. Even though He had every right to pour out His wrath on us, He poured it out on something and then someone else to give us access to Him. His only repeated command in this process was keep the fire burning; do not let it go out. In this He says, "I love you too much to lose connection with you. My love for you burns. I started the fire on your behalf. If you love Me, keep it burning."

IGNITION POINT 2: RECONCILIATION
ONCE AND FOR ALL

Atonement means reconciliation with God ultimately through Christ, so when God allowed for atonement, He was doing it Himself. From 2 Corinthians 5:19 we see that it was God's desire to bring us back to Him: "For God was in Christ, reconciling the world to himself." He understood the dire nature of our state. Because we do not have the power on our own to come to Him, He came to us:

> For God made Christ, who never sinned, to be the offering for our sin, so that we could be made right with God through Christ.
>
> —2 CORINTHIANS 5:21

Back then and at the time of Christ, God created ways to absolve us of the eternal punishment for the sin we committed and the covenant we broke. He did this despite our continual rejection of Him. God loves us so much that He made a way for us—born in sin and shaped in iniquity—to have access to Him in all His glory and holy perfection. The only requirement is that we keep the fire going.

IGNITION POINT 3: TRUE WORSHIP
AND THE JOY OF SALVATION

God has forgiven us, and we are not to forget. Our culture is so distracted by the next new thing that we begin to think our experience with God should be similar. We no longer think this salvation thing God did for us is good enough. And this is what causes our fire to die. Our minds are on so many other things that we no longer recall the significance of what He's done.

When I was growing up, the older folks used to say that if God doesn't do another thing, He's already done enough! There used to be a time when it was enough that He saved us. We could shout off of that all day. Now we respond as if He has to add all this stuff on top of it. We even make fun of someone if he starts shouting over just being saved. Is the joy of salvation not enough to set off high praise and worship? What happened to it being enough for someone to stand up and say, "When I think of the goodness of Jesus and all that He's done for me, my soul cries out"?

Because we lost sight of the Cross, our judgments of what constitutes being on fire for God are off. We judge people who shout over the seemingly simple works of God concerning our salvation, saying they are religious and emotional. But to remember that God has already done it all and all we have to do is keep it going isn't religious or emotional. We do not have to light the fire. He sent fire from heaven once and for all. All we have to do is keep it burning. When the people of God stand up and declare, "I won't forget!" more wood has been added to the fire. It is good for us to remember what the Lord has done.

The level of your passion and fire for God is directly proportionate to the level of your surrender.

When you don't feed the fire with a testimony, it dies. When you don't feed it faith, it dies. For our fire to go out means that we aren't appreciating God's love enough. Looking back at Leviticus 6, we see that each morning new wood had to be put on the fire. Tending the fire was a daily process. It wasn't about how the priest felt one day or another.

The commitment to worship God has been reduced to how we feel about the way He has blessed us. We like to decide if God is worthy of our praise this week based on how it went. Did our bosses treat us right? Did this or that go the way we wanted? This is when worship is based on feelings. This is when worship is offensive to God and He doesn't have to receive it. Have you heard of strange fire? (See Leviticus 10.) You can't offer anything to God and think He will accept it. But true worship—recounting the goodness of God and remembering the way He made it possible for you to have full access to Him—is what adds wood to the fire.

IGNITION POINT 4: SURRENDER

If you stop offering yourself to God, your fire will go out. If you stop giving Him your unconditional worship, your fire goes out. If you stop yielding certain parts of your heart to Him, your fire will go out. If you are asking God to set you on fire, but you are not feeding the fire, the fire will die. You have to feed the fire. God is not going to send fire to revive the fire. Fire doesn't revive fire. The parts of your life that need to be consumed revive the fire. When God searches your heart and shines light on certain things, release them. You are fueling the fire. When He says, "I want those thoughts, that gossip, those addictions," put them in the fire. These are the things that cause your fire to grow.

God wants to consume every part of your life. Whatever you are withholding from Him is causing your fire to die out. Revival fire burns off of your surrender. The level of your passion and fire for God is directly proportionate to the level of your surrender.

The more surrendered you are, the more passionate and on fire you will be. When you declare to God that He can have all of you, you add much fuel to the fire.

After all the years, the instruction has not changed—don't let the fire go out. The difference is that now the fire is in you. You are the keeper of the flame. God gives the fire once and says to not let it go out. We must tend to the fire.

> Let us not allow slackness to spoil our work and let us keep
> the fires of the spirit burning, as we do our work for God.
> —ROMANS 12:11, PHILLIPS

RESPOND

You want your fire to grow? Surrender. You want your fire to grow? Repent to the Lord right here and right now. Live a life of thankfulness, fall in love with the Word of the Lord, and get around people who are also on fire. If God is asking you for anything, give it to Him. I wish I could tell you that your fire will grow if you shout, but it won't. It grows by surrender. I wish I could tell you that the fire grows by dancing, but that is only a manifestation of being on fire. The fire grows by repentance. When God shows you an area in your life that is incongruent with His will and His heart, cast it off and throw it on the fire. Let God take it from you. When you do this, you are tending the fire.

Show me a surrendered, repentant people, a people who are in love with the Word, a people who are grateful for salvation, redemption, and mercy, and I'll show you a fire burning. They are not after money, houses, and cars, but they are after the grace of God. Those are a people on fire. God is setting fires in America right now, and He is telling us not to let the fire go out. Your fire will be stoked the most as you get on your face before God.

If it is your heart's desire to keep your fire burning, join me in this prayer:

> God, search me, and if You find anything in me that is incongruent with Your will, take it out of me. Forgive me. I repent. I come to You. I am hungry for You. I am desperate for You. I want You more than anything else.

Every time you pray this, you are putting wood on the fire. Paul says, "I beseech you therefore, brethren, by the mercies of God, that you present your bodies a living sacrifice, holy, acceptable to God, which is your reasonable service [or 'worship' in some translations]" (Rom. 12:1, NKJV). In other words, this is truly the way to worship God. If you really want to worship God, throw anything in you that is not like Him into the fire.

CHAPTER 13

IT HAPPENED BECAUSE
IT'S HAPPENING

"No weapon formed against you shall prosper, and every tongue which rises against you in judgment you shall condemn. This is the heritage of the servants of the LORD, and their righteousness is from Me," says the LORD.

—ISAIAH 54:17, NKJV

OWARD THE END of the first year after it had become clear God was doing something significant among us at Deeper Fellowship, the enemy began to attack many of our members and their families. There were also attacks on the city itself.

On June 12, 2016, a gunman opened fire in Pulse nightclub in Orlando, taking the lives of forty-nine people. At the time, it was named the deadliest mass shooting in modern US history. We were devastated. As the whole city mourned the losses, evidence of kindness, love, and resilience rose to the surface through first responders' and trauma surgeons' tireless efforts, long lines of people waiting to give blood to the injured survivors, all-night prayer services and vigils, and financial donations to support the victims' families.[1]

What happened in our city was unfortunate, tragic, and terroristic—a horrific act. But even in the midst of this tragedy and the many other attacks around the city and against our own members, God began to give us spiritual revelation about why the attacks—both personal and collective—were happening in this season. And what He told us, as I have said about everything up to this point, was not just for us.

The enemy wants to keep any fire of revival from burning. I want you to know that while he may try to come against you, he will not succeed. Do not be discouraged by the attacks because the enemy has overplayed his hand. Whatever the enemy has thrown and is throwing against your life and your region in this season, I declare to you, it won't work. No weapon formed against you will prosper (Isa. 54:17).

ELEVATE YOUR PERSPECTIVE

If you recall, in 1 Corinthians 2 Paul wrote about the different ways he communicated the mysteries of the gospel to different groups of people with varying levels of understanding. He wrote:

> God revealed these things by his Spirit. For his Spirit searches out everything and shows us God's deep secrets. No one can know a person's thoughts except that person's own spirit, and no one can know God's thoughts except God's own Spirit. And we have received God's Spirit (not the world's spirit), so we can know the wonderful things God has freely given us.
>
> When we tell you these things, we do not use words that come from human wisdom. Instead, we speak words given to us by the Spirit, using the Spirit's words to explain spiritual truths. But people who aren't spiritual can't receive these truths from God's Spirit. It all sounds foolish to them and they can't understand it, for only those who are spiritual can understand what the Spirit means.
>
> — 1 CORINTHIANS 2:10–14

Paul is telling us there are some things that carry a deeper spiritual meaning that goes beyond our natural understanding, and the only way to get that understanding is through a revelation from the Spirit of God. I believe that what our city and our church community were experiencing in the natural went beyond what we could see on the surface. The attacks you face as you cry out to God for more also have deeper spiritual meaning. Natural things sometimes have spiritual roots, and it's incumbent upon those of us who have spiritual insight and a prophetic eye to give a spiritual perspective of the natural things that take place. Otherwise some of us will walk around confused, and that's what the enemy wants. If the Lord gives me any revelation into a situation, I refuse to allow people to be confused about how things happening in the spirit realm are affecting things in the natural. The attacks that come in revival seasons are natural manifestations of spiritual things.

When attacks come, some people allow the enemy to lead them down the religious route of judgment and condemnation. But others desire to speak words of comfort, hope, affirmation, and life. This is the path we have chosen at Deeper. We seek to be comforters.

Times of hurt, loss, and tragedy are amazing opportunities for us to allow God's Spirit to work through us and reveal who Jesus is. We also have the opportunity to reveal the deeper prophetic understanding of the enemy's attacks. We cannot afford to be deceived. We try to find all kinds of reasons to explain the inexplicable things that happen in our lives and communities, but we must recognize that they are spiritual attacks first with natural manifestations.

Do not be discouraged by these attacks because the enemy has overplayed His hand.

People get sick, people get injured, and people die. These things are hugely unfortunate and painful for us to endure. But here's what I need you to understand: the devil doesn't play fair. You must learn to see these things for what they are—attacks from an enemy that knows he's in trouble. I am in no way ignoring the natural ramifications of pain and loss. What I hope to do is encourage those of us who are praying for revival and experiencing opposition in our homes, churches, and communities to do as Paul said and, in a manner of speaking, "elevate all things" to a spiritual level so we'll know how to stand against them.

I made this clear to our church in a sermon the weekend following the Pulse shooting—and this applies to all who are beginning to see that it's happening: we are at a critical moment because there is a demon spirit that is angry with the church. But just as his strike against us is swift and intense, so will his loss be.

TRAGEDY WILL NOT DEFINE YOU

The enemy is attempting to redefine you by your tragedy. He is attempting to silence your prophetic voice that cries out, "Thus saith the Lord." He attempted this with us in Orlando. People all over the world were asking, "What's happening in Orlando? Why is that city being attacked so badly?" Of course there were the standard speculations. But I believe we were attacked like that because "it's happening." There's a revival breaking out in our city. God is about to pour out His Spirit in an unprecedented manner in our city and from our city to the rest of the nation. So for everyone who asked what's happening in Orlando, my response was, "A revival." We aren't the only ones. There are other churches in the city that have been experiencing an outpouring of the Spirit of God as well. God is moving in our city, and the devil doesn't like it. God is moving in your life, and he doesn't like that either.

Some of the attacks happening in the body of Christ—in your life and mine—are happening because revival is happening. Revival is here, and it won't be stopped by what happened. Will you say this aloud in agreement with me? "It happened because it's happening, but what happened won't stop what's happening." It's a little bit of a tongue twister, I know, but say it loud and put it out in the atmosphere even if you don't fully understand it right now. This chapter will help you understand. The plans of the enemy won't work. They will not stop the move of God.

- -

Stories
of the River

One of the reasons we chronicle the numerous healings that have taken place at our church is because over time it's easy to forget what has happened, especially as the number of miracles increases. Of course the individuals healed will never forget, and those who knew them when they were sick will never forget. When a family member or friend no longer has cancer or can now walk without a walker or cane, you don't quickly forget. You remember things like that.

Yet sometimes things happen that no one can forget. That's what happened on a Sunday morning during River 1. The presence of God was evident in the room. There are times when it just seems as if everyone is aware of Him, and this was one of those moments. We also had the sense that God wanted to move in the room, and we specifically called out those who were dealing with certain sicknesses. I noticed in front of me a man who is normally active during worship but on this particular Sunday was sitting for most of it.

At first I wasn't sure why he was sitting so much during worship, but then I noticed a walking boot on his foot. Clearly something was wrong with his foot, and he seemed to be in a lot of pain, but when I invited people who were sick to receive prayer, he didn't come forward.

We prayed for those who came to the altar, and as we were about to move into another part of the service, out of compassion I went to him and asked what was wrong. He explained that he had broken his foot that week and would have to wear that walking boot for several weeks. Although he was in a lot of pain, he said he didn't come forward because he knew there were people who had much more serious conditions than a broken bone in their foot. He had been present for many of the other miracles that had taken place, so he said he wanted others to receive prayer.

I let him know that the Lord cared for his situation just as much as He cared for those with more serious health issues. I asked him if I could pray for him, and he said yes, so we began to pray. Sometimes when I pray for people, I feel heat in the affected area as well as in my hand. Oftentimes those who are standing around can feel it as well. I began to experience this manifestation of heat as I

prayed for the man. What happened next is something I won't soon forget, and I don't think anyone
else there that day will soon forget it either. I asked
him, "What do you feel?" He shouted, "It's gone!" A
little startled by his proclamation, I said, "What's
gone?" He said, "The pain!" Then, unprompted, he
took off his walking boot and proceeded to run
back and forth, even high-stepping. He never had
to wear the boot again. He came back the next
week in dress shoes. Jesus healed him instantly!
It's happening!

What's Happening in Orlando...Again?

There are spirits that linger over regions. We see proof of this in the
book of Daniel, when Daniel prayed and asked God to give him an
answer to something. God released the answer right away, but it took
twenty-one days for God's response to reach Daniel because a principality called the prince of Persia had been blocking it. The archangel
Michael had been fighting the demon prince for three weeks trying to
get the answer to Daniel.

Just as the prince of Persia governed a region, there are demonic
principalities that govern people's behavior and thought processes.
That's why the Bible says the weapons of our warfare are not carnal but
mighty through God to the pulling down of strongholds (2 Cor. 10:4–
5). What's a stronghold? It's a fortified thought—a thought that you
defend vehemently and can't break through even when things come to
convince you otherwise. Until a person hears and really receives the
truth of God's Word, he can't change a stronghold even if he wants to.

> It happened because it's happening, but what happened won't
> stop what's happening.

For example, poverty is a stronghold. When you see generation
after generation in poverty, and no matter how good their jobs are or
how much money they make, they're still in poverty, they're dealing

with a stronghold. It may be affecting how they respond to wisdom regarding the life choices they make or perhaps how they see their value. However it manifests, a stronghold is a deep-abiding dysfunctional mind-set. Sometimes this is called a generational curse. But it's not just a generational curse; it's also a stronghold.

There is a stronghold that hangs over the city of Orlando. If you look at the history of our city, you'll discover that three times in the last twenty-six years the fastest-growing church in America was in Orlando, yet none of them were able to sustain the momentum. It doesn't really make logical sense until you recognize that it's a spirit. Some have called this region a "pastor's graveyard." Church leaders have risen to national prominence, only to have their life and influence cut short by untimely death, drug abuse, and other sorts of scandals. There is a principality that fights the church in this region, but it is losing ground now. So when people ask what's happening in Orlando, instead of allowing us to be defined by the tragedies, I respond in the faith of "it's happening" and say, "Revival!"

Although this spirit is losing ground, it works hard to resist us, to oppose those who would actually go hard after God. I was telling someone the other day that around the time when God called me to plant Deeper Fellowship Church, I had a visitation from a demonic presence that told me if I planted a church in this city, it would take my family. The devil is a liar. This spirit took me on a journey to different churches, and it said, "See what I did there to that church? See what I did to that pastor? See how he had an affair, and now the church is a shell of its former self or is gone altogether? Do you see what I did to this church over here? Do you see how this happened? Do you see how that happened?" He said, "I'm going to do it all to you too."

No, he's not. And let me just say, this is a good reminder of why we all should pray for our pastors. This spirit was trying to persuade me to take my gifts of worship leading and prophetic insight to another city to join with somebody else rather than stand on my own. But what he didn't count on was the fact that God was sending others to stand with me. I do not stand on my own. God has equipped me and has allowed me to link arms with others who are strong in the faith to keep me and others from falling. And by God's grace, through this book and your bearing witness to what's happening in our church, the same will happen in your life and in your church and all over this nation. Miracles, signs, wonders, healing, breakthrough, deliverance, presence, worship—may it all be released everywhere that's desperately crying for more.

The enemy may have tried to take captive what God was doing, but it won't work. We are reclaiming every territory the devil has sought to destroy. We are pursuing him and recovering everything that's been taken!

Conquering the Spirit of Goliath

There are many lessons from the life of David that have influenced my worship and my warfare while contending for the presence of God to rest on me. David's encounter with the Philistine warrior Goliath gives us much to glean.

In 1 Samuel 17, when David was still newly and secretly anointed to be Israel's next king, he was out on the battlefield bringing food to his brothers. They were soldiers in King Saul's army. All of a sudden, David heard a nine-foot-tall Philistine defying the armies of the living God. This is the epitome of a spirit of intimidation—a spirit that was so confident in its ability to control the move of God that it challenged the people of God.

For forty days Goliath challenged the armies of Israel. He symbolizes a type of principality that stands over a region saying, "I can do this to you, and I can do that to you. Look at what I did to them. Do you see the size of my sword and my shield? Do you see how big and bad I am?" David said, "Who is this pagan Philistine anyway, that he is allowed to defy the armies of the living God?"

Talking all this noise, Goliath did not consider that somebody in the group would actually have faith in God. He had completely miscalculated. While he thought he was coming against the armies of Saul, David corrected that perspective by declaring that Goliath had come against the armies of the living God.

The spirit of Goliath always miscalculates and misinterprets who he is up against. In trying to come against the people of God, he is also coming against God. We serve an undefeated God who answers the cries of His people. So when we say, "We want You," He moves everything, including a principality, to get to us.

David did not think for a moment that he was fighting Goliath. He always knew Goliath was fighting God. Goliath was not only the physical manifestation of the man who stood in front of David that day. Goliath represents anything that stands against the move of God and tries to stop it through fear and intimidation.

That's what has been happening in Orlando in this new season of revival. But Goliath has it wrong. He keeps looking down on our churches that are not full, just as he mocked David's comparatively small stature, saying, "I'm still winning." But there's a remnant of people like David who will cut off Goliath's head. It has nothing to do with whether the church is full; it has everything to do with faith in God. The churches will fill up, and even when they do, our strength will still be in our faith in God, not the size of our congregations.

> *Goliath is anything that stands against the move of God and tries to stop it through fear and intimidation.*

Can I tell you something the Lord has revealed to me? God has quietly been anointing a Davidic generation in our city and around the world. He's been anointing them, He's been sending them, He's been raising them up, and they've been coming forth. They have the word of the Lord in their mouths and faith in their hearts, and they believe God can do anything. They are confident that anything that tries to oppose God will not succeed. They don't care about the statistics or what people have heard about their cities. They know their God, and they will rise up as David did and cut off the head of Goliath.

PURSUE AND RECOVER ALL

The next experience from the life of David that gives us instruction for warfare during revival is his experience at Ziklag. (See 1 Samuel

29–30.) This probably was the worst day of David's life up to that point. Being a father, husband, and pastor, I can't imagine the loss David felt that day. He had lost it all, including his family—or so it seemed.

After David's victories over the Philistines, King Saul grew more jealous of him as the days went on. His jealousy had increased so much that he was relentlessly pursuing David to kill him. To find safety from Saul's constant attacks, David went to the land of the enemy, the Philistines, and he made a deal with their king, Achish. Achish gave him a town called Ziklag. He lived fairly peacefully there until the Philistines asked him to fight with them against his own brothers, the Israelites. And David was going to do it!

Beware of the false-unity trick.

As we are seeking to keep our thoughts elevated to see the spiritual roots of the natural attacks we face, consider this: we have to be careful about joining in with calls for unity in the midst of certain troubles and tragedies. Sometimes the calls for unity also mean you must be silent about what the Lord is showing you concerning the situation. By joining the Philistines, David was choosing to oppose the armies of the Lord. There is no other way to see it. Sometimes the call for unity is a trick of the enemy meant to bring the church into a stupor so we will not speak the word of the Lord.

At every turn the enemy seeks to silence the prophetic voice of the Lord in order to redefine what God is doing. He doesn't want revival to break out, but his plans will not work! While we always must walk in love and compassion, we should never choose to be unified with the world at the expense of standing for God. Unity with the world will never work because there will always be some who don't trust or like us. We spend too much time trying to be liked by the world. Jesus said, "You will be hated by everyone because of me" (Matt. 10:22, NIV). His words were not ambiguous. The only way to be liked by the world is to deny Christ.

I know that's a little hard to hear, but the better place is to stand with Christ. The enemy is about to be sent on the run for good.

Watch out for the sneak attack.

The leaders of the Philistine army could not come to terms with David's choice to fight with them. So they sent him and his men back to Ziklag. Three days later, when David and his men arrived home, they found that the Amalekites raided the town, burned it to the ground, and took all their possessions and the women and children captive. But wait a minute. Wasn't the war between the children of Israel and the Philistines? Where did the Amalekites come from?

For a long time you've been battling one spirit, and out of nowhere, it seems, here comes a surprise attack. It's been happening to us throughout the season of revival. Remember what I had you say earlier in the chapter: it happened because it's happening, but what happened won't change what's happening.

The only way to be liked by the world is to deny Christ.

If you want to know the reason for these attacks, they are acts of retaliation. The enemy knows he's losing ground, so he is calling in reinforcements, hoping to crush us in our moments of pressure, grief, worry, and weakness. But we will not stay there because we know how to get out of the place of pressure and grief. I told our church and all who listened on the podcast the week after the Pulse shooting that what happened in our city was horrific, but we are sending that foreign demonic spirit on the run.

The enemy has been after the seed of revival in our city, so he tried to take what is valuable to us captive. But he can't kill it. We are the only ones who can kill the revival.

If you want God, you'll have Him because we are under an open heaven, we are in a season of habitation, and we are in a season of visitation—and it's available to everyone. The enemy can't kill that, but he will try to carry it away captive. And as David and his men did, we weep over what we lost until we can't weep anymore. But then something shifts.

"Bring me the ephod!"

In the midst of all of his grief, confusion, hurt, and defeat, David said, "Bring me the ephod!" (1 Sam. 30:7). The ephod is a sacred garment that only the high priest or a king could wear. It had something called the Urim and the Thummim inside the breastplate. When the people of Israel needed an answer to a major question, the priest or king would bring out the Urim and the Thummim, and it would tell them yes or no. In this particular instance when David called for the ephod, the Bible does not actually record that he pulled out the Urim and the Thummim. It seems David put the question before God. He used the ephod not only as a priestly garment but also as a garment for worship, for invoking the presence of God. For David to get the right perspective, he knew he needed to change his posture.

You know why the enemy is going to be on the run in our city, in your life, and in mine? Because we're not coming at this thing like warriors; we're coming at it like worshippers. We have to change our position and our perspective. Going forward, David knew he needed to approach God like a worshipper, not a warrior. To get the will and counsel of God, he had to get into the presence of God.

PURSUE AND RECOVER ALL

David sought the Lord. In 1 Samuel 30:8 he asked, "Should I chase after this band of raiders? Will I catch them?" The Lord told him, "Yes, go after them. You will surely recover everything that was taken from you!" (v. 8). The New King James Version says, "Pursue, for you shall surely overtake them and without fail recover all." I need you to hear the word of the Lord: you will surely recover everything that was taken from you—without fail!

A foreign enemy came into our territory and took captive what God has given us, and when we get into the presence of God, we discover the counsel of God. Some of us get into the presence of the twenty-four-hour news cycles and social media posts. Sometimes we stand on everybody else's platform and neglect the presence of God. But no more. We know what to do. We must say, "God, what should we do about this?" It may be popular in some circles to just hold each other and say, "We'll get through this." We have hashtags and memes for every sort of disaster and trauma that comes against us. But the word of the Lord is not to just stand there and take it. The word of the Lord is that we're supposed to pursue and recover all.

We will not sit by while the enemy comes in and steals the seat of revival and while he takes captive what we've been praying and laboring for.

God has shown us clearly why He is doing what He is doing here in Orlando. Think about this: Orlando is the number five most visited city in the United States.[2] Sixty-eight million people came here in 2016, a record high, and more than two million people live here.[3] Can you imagine what would happen if a full-on revival were to break out here? News of it would spread around the world. The enemy doesn't want people to come to Orlando because revival is happening here. And though he sent and keeps sending bands of raiders to take captive things that are precious to us, we will not stop contending for what belongs to us. We will not stop until we recover all.

We're not coming at this thing like warriors; we're coming at it like worshippers.

When David and his group went out to fight, the Bible says that two hundred of them were too tired to go (v. 10). It's all right if some are battle weary. They'll still get the victory. As the four hundred went on, they came upon an Egyptian slave who had been among the Amalekites. They fed him and let him rest under their protection. After he regained his strength, he led them to the camp of the enemy, and David and his men overtook them and got back everything and everyone who was stolen.

THE OPPOSITE EFFECT

I want to share another part of this spiritual warfare concept we are discussing. Just as the enemy sends these attacks to stop the move of God and get us off track, God always has a way of turning these things around and using them for His glory. David's rebound at Ziklag will forever be the testimony of one who "strengthened himself in the Lord," who changed his posture from warrior to worshipper, and who fearlessly obeyed the Lord, pursued the enemy, and recovered all. The testimony that rises to the surface despite the enemy's efforts is that God is undefeated; He always wins.

The enemy meant for the attack to kill you, but it's about to bring life. He meant for it to stop you, but it's about to bring revival. Things look one way, but that's not the way it's going to end. God is going to turn the situation around and use it for His glory. The attack of the enemy is having the opposite effect. Let me show you how I know this is true.

In Acts 28 we read about a time when the apostle Paul was on the island of Malta. He had been shipwrecked. The natives of the island were kind and had started a fire to keep their new guests warm. Wanting to keep the fire burning, Paul had collected some wood and put it on the fire. Because of the heat, a snake came out of the fire and bit Paul on the hand. The people of the island saw it hanging from his hand and thought he was attacked because of something bad he had done—"A murderer, no doubt!" (v. 4). But Paul just shook the snake off and kept going.

> *The devil thinks he can outlast this generation, but we are going to strike until we see revival happening everywhere!*

The people looked on, waiting for him to swell up and die. The longer they looked, the more they realized there was something different about Paul. They expected the injury to cause him to drop dead at any moment. Not only did he not die, but also there was no sign of the attack. After witnessing this, the people were in awe.

Then Paul went in and prayed for the sick father of the chief of the island, and he was healed. And not only that; Paul prayed for everyone who was sick, and they also were healed. Because of the miraculous work of God, when it was time for Paul and his company to leave, the people showered them with honors and all the supplies they needed.

I declare to you that the same thing that happened to Paul will happen to you. The attack of the enemy will have the opposite effect on your life. When the enemy strikes, some will be waiting for your demise, but they are about to be shocked. There are those who are waiting for you to quit, give up, throw in the towel, but they are going to be shocked. Yes, the enemy bit you, but you will not die. You will live and proclaim the works of the Lord (Ps. 118:17). You are still here! You have confused the enemy by the way you have come back from his attacks. He thought he could take you out, but you shook him off and threw him in the fire.

Your resilience is about to change your family, city, and nation. Your resilience is about to start a wildfire. The people of the island ended up wanting what Paul had. Whatever kept him from going under when the enemy attacked him they wanted. Since it didn't kill him, they believed that if they had whatever he had, they also wouldn't die if attacked. And what happened next is what I declare is going to happen in the season of attack: the enemy's assault on your life is about to cause a revival in all those who know you. The enemy messed up when he showed his head and attacked you.

HOW WORSHIPPERS WAGE WAR

So I'm saying this to you and to the spirits that have ruled in our homes and geographic regions for far too long: we will not give in to the attacks. We will pursue and recover all that we've prayed and labored for. We wage war, but not like the world wages war, for the weapons of our warfare are not carnal, but they are mighty through God to the pulling down of strongholds. We are taking up our positions as worshippers, as those who seek the presence of the Lord. And we will see these attacks thrown into the fire to fuel the revival we are crying out for. The enemy's attacks will not end with our disgrace, defeat, or death. They will end with the name of the Lord glorified forever.

So if people ask you what's happening in your life, church, or city, do not define yourself by any of the trials and tragedies you're facing or that are taking place around you. Tell them as we do at Deeper

Fellowship that a revival is what's happening, and you will not stop until the whole world knows about it.

RESPOND

I want to challenge you to consider your posture as this move of God spreads around the world. Consider how you are approaching the attacks that come into your life. Are you taking up the posture of a warrior? Or are you taking the posture of a worshipper? Worshippers know where to be when the heat is turned up. Worshippers know that sounds get God's attention. Worshippers are the ones who say in the midst of the valley of the shadow of death, "Bring me the ephod!"

The devil thinks he can outlast this generation, but we're not going to stop until we see revival happening everywhere. One of my favorite examples of what it will take for us to keep the fire burning and the enemy at bay is found in 2 Kings 13:18–19. An enemy was coming against the children of Israel again. From the prophet Elisha's house they could see the enemy charging toward them. The Bible says:

> Then [Elisha] said, "Now pick up the other arrows and strike them against the ground." So the king [Jehoash] picked them up and struck the ground three times. But the man of God was angry with him. "You should have struck the ground five or six times!" he exclaimed. "Then you would have beaten Aram until it was entirely destroyed. Now you will be victorious only three times."

The message here is strike until. Don't relent. Don't hesitate. Keep praying until you see the answer manifest. Keep testifying until salvation comes to your family. Keep worshipping until you see breakthrough. Don't stop until the enemy is destroyed. Strike until you have recovered all!

CHAPTER 14

LIVING STONES

Each of you must pick up one stone and carry it out on your shoulder—twelve stones in all, one for each of the twelve tribes of Israel. We will use these stones to build a memorial....He did this so all the nations of the earth might know that the LORD's hand is powerful, and so you might fear the LORD your God forever.

—JOSHUA 4:5-6, 24

T IS HARD to believe that I have lived to see the moment I prayed for—we prayed for—for years. Some have prayed for forty years. Others, forty days. And still others may have just joined in the last forty minutes. Yet we all will be recipients of the residual effects of God's answering all the prayers from all the hearts of people across the globe. What we are seeing happen in this moment in time is sovereignly orchestrated. It is something only God can do. He's brought all the prayers together and by His will is changing our destinies and making us part of something that will outlast all of us.

When the Lord walks into a room to mark a people, as He did for us at Deeper, He does so to mark them in a way that allows them to hear from Him supernatural things that are too big for the human mind to receive without His presence. Since the moment He walked into Deeper, everything about how we do what we do has changed. Prior to that moment we were teaching in series and layering prophetic thoughts and prophesying about a future that was to come, not knowing that the future that was to come was right upon us. We were believing God and making declarations of things that seemed to be far into the future. We essentially assumed the things we were talking about probably wouldn't manifest to us in our building but would manifest through us in some distant way. But God said, "No, I want to do it through you, and I want to do it now."

The amazing thing about trying to "prepare" for a moment like that is that encounters don't come at your choosing. By definition an encounter is an unexpected meeting. God chooses the encounter. All we can do is be in position for one. And ultimately we found ourselves continually in a position of crying out to God.

I don't know about anyone else who has experienced something like this, but I didn't know when to expect it. Almost two decades ago I read a book called *The God Chasers* by Tommy Tenney. When I finished it, I put the book down and said, "God, for the rest of my life I won't rest until I have an encounter like this." Since then every time I have led worship anywhere around the world, I have led trying to position those of us in the room for an encounter. I looked at every single moment, every single service, wondering, "Could this be the moment? Could this be the moment God walks in?" After living every day of the last twenty or so years with that kind of anticipation, what the Lord did in one moment during our service on May 22, 2016—that was sudden.

A year later the Lord led us to hold a special service acknowledging how that moment changed us. We could not move on as if nothing happened. More than two hundred miracles have taken place since the moment the Lord walked into the room, and it wasn't because we call ourselves a healing ministry or were having healing crusades. The miracles aren't taking place because we are constantly saying, "Bring the sick and the lame, and we'll pray for them and lay hands on them." Most of the miracles taking place happen because the Lord Himself does it, and even some of those happen for people who are not in the room. People of faith place on the altar the names of individuals who are not in the room but need a special touch from God, and they receive it wherever they are in the world.

One year into our revival experience with God we could not do anything but stop and thank Him. It was not about trying to re-create the moment He walked in the room. It was about our honoring what He did. In essence, we were saying, "God, we're not going to let the day or the moment pass by and act as if You didn't show up and change us forever." We stopped to acknowledge that we were not the same anymore.

"God, for the rest of my life, I won't rest until I have an encounter like this."

Any people who have had an encounter with the living God should mark it and acknowledge what God has done. As they did for the men and women of old, these times of acknowledgment serve as lasting memorials, living stones to honor the presence of God in our lives.

MARKED FOR LIFE

I have a little scar on my left eye. It wasn't until my children became fascinated by it that I remembered it was there. What I haven't forgotten is how I got it. When I was a young boy, I used to go to North Carolina every summer to spend time with my grandparents and my cousins. Wrestling was a big deal back then. It may be a big deal for people now, but this was the era of the classic "yellow trunks" Hulk Hogan, not the "bad" Hulk Hogan, which he turned into later. Wrestling was in its prime, and my cousins and I watched it all the time.

Of course we would try to imitate the moves. There was one move called the "monkey flip," which my older cousin thought would be the perfect one to try out on me. I don't know how it happened, but I was the guinea pig for everything. So he said, "Hey, let's try the monkey flip!" He flipped me, and when I landed, things got quiet for a second. Then I had this overwhelming sense of peace and calm and warmth. But it wasn't the Holy Spirit. I didn't feel any pain, but I remember looking up and seeing a panicked, horrified look on my cousin's face.

Someone said, "Shh! Be quiet! Shh, shh! Be quiet!"

I was thinking, "What's going on?"

My cousin took his hand and wiped my face. Then he wiped his hand on the carpet, I saw his handprint in my blood, and I started screaming.

My grandmother called out from somewhere else in the house, "What's going on?"

My cousin was still saying, "Shh! Shh! Be quiet! Be quiet!"

I screamed and hollered.

My grandmother came in and noticed the big gash on my head. There was some fuss and commotion before my aunt rushed me to the hospital. It's funny that my biggest fear in that whole situation wasn't the blood; it was getting stitches. I'm pain adverse, thanks to my mother, who has a unique gift for describing painful things in such a way that you feel the pain as she talks. So I was terrified on the way to the emergency room. When the doctor confirmed that I would need stitches, my aunt told me that I said, "No! Let the Lord heal it!" I believed in the power of God even at ten years old.

So, a few stitches and thirty-plus years later, I have a scar that I don't even think about until my daughter crawls up in my lap and asks, "What's that?" And I tell her the monkey-flip story for the nth time. The scar marks a moment from my past.

Whenever we go through something traumatic, there's typically something that will remind us of it. It could be a scar or a sound or a smell, but it marks that experience forever. Whenever something amazing happens, there's typically something that causes us to remember, and again we are marked forever. Either by chance or intention, there are markers that lead us to remember past events. But there is absolutely nothing in the world that marks us like an encounter with God, and God wants us to remember those moments.

BUILD A MEMORIAL

In Joshua 4 we happen upon a significant moment in the life of the children of Israel. Their story as a nation began with God prophetically revealing to Abraham the destiny of his seed. He said that they would be in bondage for four hundred years, and they were. (See Genesis 15.) They cried out to the Lord for deliverance, and God raised up Moses to lead them out of bondage in Egypt. (See Exodus 3.) At first, Pharaoh wouldn't set them free, as the Lord hardened his heart. (See Exodus 9:12.) But finally they were released into the wilderness with gold, silver, and everything they needed for going into the Promised Land. (See Exodus 14.)

You know God has done something significant when you remember exactly when it happened.

The only thing they lacked was enough faith to get there. So they grumbled and complained, making their time in the wilderness much longer and more arduous than God had intended. Because of this, an entire generation died in the wilderness under Moses's leadership. (See Numbers 14.) Moses also transgressed against God and was not allowed to go into the Promised Land. (See Numbers 20:12.)

In Moses's place God raised up Joshua and commissioned him to take the next generation into the Promised Land. (See Joshua 1.) Joshua 4 chronicles the moment when this new generation, who had survived the wilderness, crossed the Red Sea and the Jordan River to enter the Promised Land. But before they took possession of the promise, God had them stop and remember "the tenth day of the first month" (v. 19), the day the people of Israel "crossed the Jordan on dry ground" (v. 22).

This was a significant moment—a pivotal, life-altering encounter remembered with specificity. You know God has done something significant when you remember exactly when it happened. This is why we continue to remember that significant, pivotal, life-altering encounter that took place May 22, 2016. The date is not significant for everyone. Everyone was not in church on that day. Some of the people who've joined us since then missed that moment. But it was important enough to us to mark it.

God has a specific purpose for each memory. God instructed the people of Israel to make a memorial so future generations would also know what God did. In Joshua 4 two reasons rise to the surface for why God also wants us to build memorials for the things He has done: 1) for our children and future generations to know His goodness (Josh. 4:6–7, 21–22); 2) and so all the nations of the earth might know how powerful He is (Josh. 4:24).

A MEMORY IS NOT ONLY FOR YOU; IT'S FOR THE FUTURE

The only way an encounter will outlive you is for you to mark it. Otherwise it will die with you. You don't want encounters to die with you. This is why God instructs us to make a memorial. Not only is what we experience with God for us right now, but it is also for our children.

God says to us in Deuteronomy 4:9:

> But watch out! Be careful never to forget what you yourself have seen. Do not let these memories escape from your mind as long as you live! And be sure to pass them on to your children and grandchildren.

This is a command of the Lord. If you're a parent and you're not rehearsing the goodness of God with your children, you're doing them a disservice, and you're disobeying the Word of the Lord. When God does something for you, tell them, even if you consider it to be small. If you didn't know how you were going to make it till the end of the month and the Lord provided, tell them. You keep waiting for big things such as, "My leg got chopped off, it grew back, and God did it." No, no, no. If you had more month than money and God made the money come together, tell your children what the Lord has done.

> Listen, O Israel! The LORD is our God, the LORD alone. And you must love the LORD your God with all your heart, all your soul, and all your strength. And you must commit yourselves wholeheartedly to these commands that I am giving you today. Repeat them again and again to your children. Talk about them when you are at home and when

you are on the road, when you are going to bed and when you are getting up. Tie them to your hands and wear them on the forehead as reminders. Write them on the doorposts of your house and on your gates.

—DEUTERONOMY 6:4–9

Don't stay silent about the goodness of the Lord to your children. That is a command of the Lord.

Stories
of the River

During the Habitation Conference we host every September, we always experience a near-indescribable encounter with God. People come from around the world to be immersed in an encounter with God for days. In 2017 when we opened registration, the conference sold out in less than ten hours. People who are hungry for a move of God literally converge in Orlando from around the globe.

During the gathering in 2017 the Holy Spirit led me to share several of the things that had been taking place in our midst because one of the things I understand about a testimony is that it creates faith for the future! The telling of a testimony creates room for God to do it again.

After I shared testimonies of healing during one of the morning sessions, faith for healing was strong in the atmosphere, and we began to pray. We are still receiving testimonies about what God did that day. We've received testimonies of breast cancer healed, a deaf ear opened, and lupus healed, and we saw two people walk without their walkers. My good friend Jordan also was healed of a rotator cuff injury.

He had learned to deal with the pain over time, but he knew the injury would one day need to be surgically addressed. Jordan wasn't one of the people who came down to receive prayer. In fact, he didn't even know the Lord had healed him until he woke up in the middle of the night almost in a panic when he realized that he was sleeping on the side of his body with the injured rotator cuff. Normally if he slept on that side, he'd end up in excruciating pain.

When he realized what he'd done, he expected to experience a surge of pain, but it never came. The pain was completely gone. His range of motion was completely restored. He came up to testify about that, and while he was doing so, our music director for the conference got my attention and told me that in that moment he was healed of the same issue. Both of them demonstrated their healing by moving their arms in ways that they previously could not have without extreme pain. Both of these men were healed in the river of God without anyone laying hands on them. Jesus did it Himself. It's happening!

- -

A MEMORIAL PROVOKES A QUESTION

Throughout the Old Testament God instructed His people to build memorials. He wanted the memorials to provoke questions so the story of God's miraculous interventions would be told over and over. That's why multiple times in the Scripture, and particularly in Joshua 4, it says, "Your children will ask you." In the future when your children ask you, "What's this for?" they will have an opportunity to discover the great things God has done. When you forget what God has done and don't build a memorial, there will be no inquiry and no opportunity for faith to be built in that area.

When there's no memory of past victories, small things look big. If the Red Sea wasn't a part of the history of the children of Israel, the Jordan River would have looked insurmountable. When you forget what God has done, it causes you to question and doubt what He can do.

A MEMORIAL CREATES FAITH FOR THE FUTURE

A memorial is a witness of faith for future generations. It is a testimony to all future generations declaring what God has done while simultaneously declaring what He can and will do. This is why God says, "Talk to your children." There may come a day when you aren't there, and they need to find the faith and confidence to know that if God did this before, He can do it again. "If God did it for my mother and father, then He'll do it for me. I don't have to worry." If your testimony of faith is great, then they don't start where you started. Their faith launches from where yours stopped. Your faith ceiling is their floor.

> *When you forget what God has done and don't build a memorial, there will be no opportunity for faith to be built.*

The whole Bible is a memorial that testifies of the goodness and greatness of God. Every time we read it, it builds faith. Likewise your testimony says, "Don't expect less," and, "Don't settle for less."

Each stone that goes into building a memorial is a testimony. God told Joshua to have one man from each tribe grab a stone, signifying that no one was to be left out. No one is supposed to be left out of the move of God. You can't say it's a move of God if it leaves people out. You can't call it revival if it's exclusive. If one person from each tribe was to bring one stone, that means everyone would have been involved in building the memorial, and that is the way it was to be from generation to generation.

A STONE IS A WITNESS

May 22, 2016, changed everything in our church. This is the day the prophetic words that had been spoken over our congregation manifested before our eyes. We won't forget, and we can't forget. It is a stone for us.

The New Living Translation renders Joshua 4:6 this way: "We will use these stones to build a memorial." The New King James

Version reads, "This may be a sign among you." The translations come together to help us understand that the Israelites were building a place to remember a miracle, or they were building a place that would bear witness to the miracle that happened there. Joshua obeyed the Lord, who told them that the stones would mark that place where God performed such a mighty act of deliverance. So in essence, a memorial stone is a sign, and a sign is a witness; that means a stone is a sign, and a stone is a witness. Israel was to give a strong witness to the power of God.

Joshua 3:14–16 tells us about the miracle they were memorializing. The Bible says,

> So the people left their camp to cross the Jordan, and the priests who were carrying the Ark of the Covenant went ahead of them. It was the harvest season, and the Jordan was overflowing its banks. But as soon as the feet of the priests who were carrying the Ark touched the water at the river's edge, the water above that point began backing up a great distance away at a town called Adam, which is near Zarethan. And the water below that point flowed on to the Dead Sea until the riverbed was dry. Then all the people crossed over near the town of Jericho.

The Jordan dried up before the ark of the Lord. This is the place where God did the impossible for them, and the stones they were instructed to set as a memorial spoke to this miracle and the God of the miracle. What's even more amazing is that they were told to not get just any stones. They were to get the stones "from the very place where the priests are standing in the middle of the Jordan" (Josh. 4:3), from the "middle of the Jordan, in front of the Ark of the LORD your God" (v. 5). This was to be the empirical evidence that this miracle actually happened.

It's not a move of God if it leaves people out. You can't call it revival if it's exclusive.

This also means there are certain miracles you can only receive when you are near the presence of God. If you remember from chapter 10, the ark of the Lord represents the presence of God. There's a certain testimony that you can only get in the presence of God, in the river of God. They were standing there in the river when God moved. And guess what? Every river has stones! The only way to get stones is to be where God is moving.

YOU ARE A STONE

There are two key verses that help us see that stones are not some mysterious objects in the spirit realm that we are to somehow grab and place in an intangible location. Instead, we see that we are the stones that testify of what God has done. Stones are not ancient relics or things we can't access every day around the world at any time, perhaps like the real historical sites in Israel where the miraculous happenings we've discussed so far occurred. No. There are real and living memorials that we build every day with our own lives. We are the ones who have been in the river of God, near the presence of God, and who can be the real, empirical evidence of His powerful hand.

Here's what Jesus said in Acts 1:8:

> You will receive power when the Holy Spirit comes upon you. And you will be my witnesses, telling people about me everywhere.

Then in 1 Peter 2:4–9, specifically in verse 9, we get a deeper understanding of our purpose as living stones. The passage says:

> You are coming to Christ, who is the living cornerstone of God's temple. He was rejected by people, but he was chosen by God for great honor.
>
> And you are living stones that God is building into his spiritual temple. What's more, you are his holy priests. Through the mediation of Jesus Christ, you offer spiritual sacrifices that please God. As the Scriptures say, "I am

placing a cornerstone in Jerusalem, chosen for great honor, and anyone who trusts in him will never be disgraced."

Yes, you who trust him recognize the honor God has given him. But for those who reject him, "The stone that the builders rejected has now become the cornerstone." And, "He is the stone that makes people stumble, the rock that makes them fall."

They stumble because they do not obey God's word, and so they meet the fate that was planned for them.

But you are not like that, for you are a chosen people. You are royal priests, a holy nation, God's very own possession. As a result, you can show others the goodness of God, for he called you out of the darkness into his wonderful light.

—1 Peter 2:4–9

This is the purpose of stones: "you can show others the goodness of God, for he called you out of the darkness into his wonderful light." In other words, living stones have a job description.

Your Job Description

I love the way *The Message* translates 1 Peter 2:9–10. It says,

> But you are the ones chosen by God, chosen for the high calling of priestly work, chosen to be a holy people, God's instruments to do his work and speak out for him, to tell others of the night-and-day difference he made for you— from nothing to something, from rejected to accepted.

Do you wonder why we keep talking about our encounters? It's because we have a job description. We are living stones, and our job is "to do his work and speak out for him, to tell others of the night-and-day difference he made" for us. Did He take you from nothing to something and from rejected to accepted? Do you have a testimony?

Your stones of praise are markers for the power of God working in your life.

Remembering what God has done for us and constantly rehearsing His goodness in our lives becomes the fuel for our worship and passion for Him. When your children see you praise, lift your hands, bow down, shout, sing, and cry, that's a stone. When your worship gets people's attention, they are watching you say, "Let me tell you a story. This is how God found me, but now this is where I am. I was the least of these, the least qualified, the least likely to be called. But God saw something in me, and He came and rescued me."

People watching you will see how quickly you are moved to worship. They will see that it doesn't take much for you to get in His presence. And they will see that it is because of the goodness of Jesus and all that He's done for you.

Your stones of worship are a memorial set before your children, neighbors, and coworkers that will tell them of the times when God healed, delivered, and set you free. Your stones of praise are markers of the power of God working in your life. You are a living stone!

LET THE ROCKS CRY OUT

There's a reason we praise, remember, and testify. Luke 19:36–40 gives us a clue:

> As he rode along, the crowds spread out their garments on the road ahead of him. When he reached the place where the road started down the Mount of Olives, all of his followers began to shout and sing as they walked along, praising God for all the wonderful miracles they had seen.
>
> "Blessings on the King who comes in the name of the LORD! Peace in heaven, and glory in highest heaven!"
>
> But some of the Pharisees among the crowd said, "Teacher, rebuke your followers for saying things like that!"
>
> He replied, "If they kept quiet, the stones along the road would burst into cheers!"

What Jesus meant here is that if His followers were to keep quiet, there would one day be a group of people on the earth who would not remain silent because their testimonies would speak. Even if

they kept quiet in His day, their silence wouldn't squelch the movement. There would be people who would know that He's been so
good that the stone of their testimonies would cry out. Jesus wasn't
talking about rocks on the ground. He was talking about people
who know who He is. He was talking about us. We are the living
stones. We are the memorials of God. We are the ones who carry
the evidence of God's power.

Cornelius asked for a river; God responded with the ocean.

Our stones are very important because they build memorials in
two places. Not only are they present with you here on earth, but
they are also building memorials for you in heaven. In Acts 10 an
angel of the Lord visited with Cornelius, a captain in the Italian
army who was also a follower of Christ. The angel told him, "Your
prayers and your alms have come up for a memorial before God."
The stone on earth is a memorial. Your prayers and your giving are
offered to your church, in your home, or in some everyday showing
of generosity, but God is keeping record of them in heaven, and
they become memorials to Him. Your stones live in two places.

But here's the amazing thing: the Bible never says what Cornelius
prayed for. This is going to blow your mind. If Ephesians 3:20 is true,
"Now unto him that is able to do exceeding abundantly above all
that we ask or think" (KJV), then this is what God did for Cornelius.
Cornelius asked for a river; God responded with the ocean.

The Bible doesn't say that Cornelius asked for the salvation of
every non-Jew for the rest of the history of the earth, but that's
what he got. If you read the rest of the account in Acts 10, you
will see that Cornelius's faithfulness caused him to be the door
through which the Gentiles were able to hear the gospel and
receive the Holy Spirit.

All this is to say that you have no idea how powerful your stones
of worship, prayer, and giving actually can be. You have no idea what
the memorial to God actually can mean. Do you want to know why
I believe the Lord decided to show up on May 22, 2016, at Deeper

Fellowship Church in Orlando, Florida? Because there is a bunch of people here who have memorials in heaven.

RESPOND

Your worship is building a memorial. My worship is building a memorial. Your testimony is building a memorial for your children and future generations. My testimony is doing the same, and even more personally, it is building a memorial for my son. Every time he asks me, "Daddy, why do you have to go on the airplane?" I don't say, "Because I have to go to work." I tell him I am getting on that plane because I am going to proclaim the gospel of Jesus Christ to other nations.

The next generation is watching us build stones in memorial to the things the Lord is doing in this season. Our intentional and deliberate marking of the goodness, presence, and power of the Lord working in our lives will fuel their passion from here to eternity. We are getting them in position for a perpetual outpouring of the Spirit of God. Our spiritual ceiling is their floor. The higher we go, the higher the platform from which they launch the next move of God.

I want to invite you to take a moment right now and recall the things the Lord has done in your life. I invite you to begin picking up another stone to add to the memorial you are building. This is one thing that God commanded that we aren't deliberate enough about. If it means that you get out your prayer journal and start to write things down, do it. Then next time the Lord gives you an opportunity to talk with your children, neighbors, friends, or coworkers, let them in on what God has done. Build your memorial one testimony at a time.

You may not have been with us on May 22, 2016, but what you're doing now is creating a new day on the calendar for when God moved in the earth. It's creating another portal and invasion of the presence of God to connect with us on earth. You're building the memorial right now for another outpouring, revelation, and visitation—another encounter with the living God.

CHAPTER 15

YOU WERE BORN FOR THIS

By the rivers of Babylon we sat and
wept when we remembered Zion.

—PSALM 137:1, NIV

BEFORE YOU WERE a thought in the minds of men, you existed in the mind of God. Before you were a twinkle in your parents' eyes, you were the apple of God's. He conceived His thoughts of you as He formed the foundations of the earth. You have been on God's mind from the beginning of time. Therefore you are not a mistake. You are not here by mistake. Your arrival here in this moment was and is intentional. If anyone has told you different, know that person can't know about you what your Creator knows. You are here by His design.

Because God knew you before you were formed in your mother's womb, it was His intentional will to send you into the earth at this specific time. Again, if you thought you were a mistake, if you were ever told you were a mistake, I need you to hear the word of the Lord: God intended for you to be here, no matter what the circumstances were that surrounded your arrival. The Lord placed you here on purpose because you have an assignment. You were born for this moment. Say it aloud right now: "I was born for this moment."

If this were not true, you could have been born at any random time, but you weren't. God intentionally set you on His time line in this generation, for this time, and for a purpose. There is something special about the verse that opens this chapter. I want you to see what it tells us about God's set time and the people He appoints to live in that time.

THE SETUP

At the time God called Jeremiah, Israel was being ruled by evil kings and false prophets. It was hard to tell the truth from a lie, the word of the Lord from the word of man. Because of this the people were confused and had been led astray. But God saw some glimpses of righteousness among His people, and He set a plan in motion to help restore them back to a people who followed hard after Him.

Declare: "I was born for this moment."

Looking for someone to be His mouthpiece and communicate His instructions, will, and thoughts to the people, He called a very young Jeremiah into His presence and appointed him to be His prophet to the nations. (See Jeremiah 1:4–10.) God forewarned Jeremiah that not everyone would like what God would say through him, but He would be with him and He would protect him. Then the Lord touched Jeremiah's mouth, gave him the words to speak, told him the plan to revive His people, and sent him out.

The first part of God's plan was to send the people into exile for seventy years. As a result, Jerusalem was destroyed. We need to understand that this was a consequence of Israel's turning their back on God, worshipping idols, and breaking their covenant with God. God does not wink at sin, particularly when His people dishonor him and allow sin to be perpetuated from generation to generation. So this was the word of the Lord spoken through the prophet Jeremiah:

> "I will banish from them the sounds of joy and gladness, the voices of bride and bridegroom, the sound of millstones and the light of the lamp. This whole country will become a desolate wasteland, and these nations will serve the king of Babylon seventy years. But when the seventy years are fulfilled, I will punish the king of Babylon and his nation, the

land of the Babylonians, for their guilt," declares the LORD, "and will make it desolate forever."

—JEREMIAH 25:10–12, NIV

Although God was going to send them into seventy years of exile, He also promised to send revival and restoration. He was letting them know that yes, they would have to deal with their sins, but afterward something big was coming.

When everything began to happen according to God's will, false prophets came forward and told the people that everything was going to be OK, that God was not angry, and that all He wanted was for them to be happy. They said it would not be seventy years of exile but only two and that God would bless them. Hananiah was one of the leading false prophets, and those who wanted a comfortable, feel-good message sided with him. Those who wanted to obey the word of the Lord submitted to what God was saying.

That's why you have to be careful not to so easily receive the words that make you feel good. In this instance Hananiah, the other false prophets, and the people who listened to the word that made them feel good were destroyed. (See Jeremiah 28.) God does some things that you may not understand or like, but He does them to protect you.

A NEW GENERATION ARISES

In Jeremiah 29 we read a letter Jeremiah sent to those in exile telling them how to maintain until the time for their deliverance comes:

> Build houses and settle down; plant gardens and eat what they produce. Marry and have sons and daughters; find wives for your sons and give your daughters in marriage, so that they too may have sons and daughters. Increase in number there; do not decrease. Also, seek the peace and prosperity of the city to which I have carried you into exile. Pray to the LORD for it, because if it prospers, you too will prosper.
>
> —JEREMIAH 29:5–7, NIV

God was letting them know that seventy years is a long time—"Settle in, get comfortable, and raise your families as you would if you were at home." He also instructed them to pray for the city they were held captive in, and this is a lesson to us as well: pray for the place that God sends you—the job, the church, the city, the assignment. Don't curse them, because if you do, their curse is your curse.

The other, more significant thing here is that because of the command to grow their families and increase in number, there would be a people, a generation, born in exile. A people born in between seasons. A people too young to experience what was, but not old enough to have become cynical about what was yet to be. The only thing the born-exiles would have was a word from the Lord about a day of restoration, a day of revival. They were not born in Jerusalem, which means they did not have a memory to think back on. All they had was the word of the Lord for their future.

BORN FOR REVIVAL

Never having seen the glory of Jerusalem, this new generation of Israelites was looking forward to something they had never seen. Having been born in captivity, born in exile, they were also born for revival. God knew when He was placing these people into this time line that some would have been born in Jerusalem and moved into exile and others would have been born in Babylon and had only the word of the Lord to hold on to.

Sometimes you find yourself in a certain season, and you don't understand why you're there. The Israelites who were born in exile weren't the ones who lived when Israel's evil king Manasseh led the nation into idolatry. They hadn't served idols. They weren't the ones who aroused God's anger. They weren't the ones who listened to the false prophets. They weren't born in Jerusalem. They had no memory of the beauty of the holy city. Yet Psalm 137 is their cry: "By the waters of Babylon, there we sat down and wept, when we remembered Zion" (v. 1, ESV).

Can you hear their heart? "I wasn't around for what it was, so I have no frame of reference, but something in me says this isn't all there is. Something in my spirit longs for a home, for a reality in the spirit that my natural eyes have yet to see, and whenever I think about it, I weep." Does this sound familiar?

WE TOO WEEP FOR ZION

If you think about it, it probably looks weird to others when they see our generation crying. It probably looks weird to others when they see us longing for something we've never seen but have only read about. We too are a generation born in between. Our eternal Father placed something in us that causes us to cry out. He put us here for this moment for a specific reason and a specific purpose because He knows that we will seek Him until we find Him. He knew we would be the generation that would cry out for something we had never seen. Why? Because there's something on the inside of us that will not be satisfied with where we are.

You may not have been in the room with us when God walked into Deeper that day, but you're still crying out with us because God wove the longing for more of Him into your DNA. He put you here in this generation because He knew you would be part of a people who would not get lazy, a people who would cry out for revival day and night, even though they've never seen it.

It's not our fault that we're here, but it is our problem. He knew that we would know Him as the problem solver, so we cry out to Him day and night. We weep whenever we think about revival and whenever we think about restoration. This is what Zion represents in Psalm 137. It says, "We sat down and we wept when we remembered Zion." Why did they weep? They wept because they were holding on to the word of the Lord that was given to them by the prophet Jeremiah: "When seventy years are completed for Babylon, I will come to you and fulfill my good promise to bring you back to this place" (Jer. 29:10, NIV). God was saying, "I will bring you home again. I will restore you." That moment of weeping signified their determination to hold on to the word of the Lord despite the current season they were in. Things looked crazy, and in the midst of the craziness they wept because they remembered that God had promised their generation would see revival.

REFUSE TO ACCEPT YOUR PRESENT CONDITIONS AS NORMAL

The key to revival is to not accept your present conditions as normal. The Israelites' present conditions were not OK. They sat by the river and wept because they realized there was something more than what they were living.

Have you ever attended one good church service after another and things were going pretty good, but something on the inside of you said, "Yeah, there's more than this"? God wants to do something through a people that affects the world. He wants it to expand out from just what's happening in a small warehouse on a corner in central Orlando. There must be a people who will be part of spreading the move of God throughout the nations of the earth. And until I see that, I can't be satisfied.

> There on the poplars we hung our harps, for there our captors asked us for songs, our tormentors demanded songs of joy; they said, "Sing us one of the songs of Zion!" How can we sing the songs of the LORD while in a foreign land?
> —PSALM 137:2–4, NIV

The tormentors are those who were keeping them in Babylon. They were basically saying, "Act as if everything is normal. Go back to doing normal things. Sings songs as if you're back in Zion." Their captors, their tormentors want them to forget revival and live in the moment, to forget that they had a promise from God. What did these exile-born Israelites even know about what Zion was like? They were born in between seasons. Their tormentors sound like some of ours: "You're doing too much. You're crying too much. You're praying too much. You're shouting too much. Just act as if everything's fine. What are you talking about, 'revival is coming'? Don't you know it's already here?"

But those born in exile were saying, "No, no, no. What we are holding on to has yet to come, but we long for it. We can't act as if everything is normal. Something on the inside says, 'It's bigger than this.'"

God has blessed Deeper Fellowship to see more than two hundred miracles, but we're not going to be satisfied with only that when we know there's more. What God wants to do is bigger than that. We're not going to be satisfied with a few songs of worship. It's bigger than that. God wants to impact the world. Don't tell this generation to be quiet. We weep and cry out because there's more! We refuse to accept our current conditions as normal.

The exile-born Israelites understood that they may not have been born in Jerusalem, but they had a promise from God about restoration and revival, so they wouldn't accept anything else as normal. In the same way, we must also resist the temptation to rush back to false normalcy. We must resist the temptation to try to act as if everything is normal when the Holy Spirit is the One who is stirring us up and making us uncomfortable. He's doing it on purpose. He's doing that so we will not try to get back to normal. He doesn't want us to get back to normal. He wants to redefine what normal is. The new normal is revival.

COMPLACENCY IS NOT NORMAL

Oftentimes we hate being uncomfortable so badly that we'll do almost anything to find comfort, including acting as if the things that hurt us don't hurt. There are moments in time when we need to allow discomfort to realign our posture. It is not normal to be complacent. It is not normal to not desire to be in God's presence. It is not normal to live as if we don't need Him. It is not normal to live in a society that turns its back on God. It's not normal to live in a society where the church is marginalized. It's not normal to live in a society where the prophetic voice is silenced and even mocked. It's not normal to live in a society where sin is celebrated and the upright are being vilified. It's not normal to live in a society where genuine love and truth are called hate. It is not normal to live in a society where the Word of God is disrespected. These things are not normal, and we need to resist allowing them to be normalized.

Allow discomfort to realign our posture.

When we see the things happening in the world, it ought to inform our cry for revival and remind us of our need for it. When you see police officers gunned down in city streets, it ought to inform our posture for revival. When we see hate groups marching around in the country, trying to make their voices heard, it ought to tell us that we need revival. When we see people who don't even know the Lord but think their marching with signs is going to change what's ailing, it ought to tell us that we need revival. We would rather pretend that everything is OK when it's not OK for the sake of normalcy, rather than face where we really are.

REVIVAL IS IN YOUR DNA

Psalm 137 continues with:

> If I forget you, Jerusalem, may my right hand forget its skill.
> May my tongue cling to the roof of my mouth if I do not
> remember you, if I do not consider Jerusalem my highest joy.
> —PSALM 137:5–6, NIV

"If I forget you" is an interesting phrase because of the two types of people who were in exile. There were those who came from Jerusalem, and there were those who had never been. So how can the ones who had never been in Jerusalem remember it? Could it be that where they were was never where they were designed to be? God is implying something significant here. Those who have experienced God—the seasoned saints—were to pass on the experience to those who had not known Jerusalem. They were to do it in a way that would cause them to long for it. This is why it's important that the mature grow up with the immature.

This is why it is important that God puts a church family together, because those who have had an encounter with God are supposed to talk about it so other people who have not had an encounter will long for it. This is what the last chapter focused on—the importance of our testimony, living stones, and setting up memorials. The mature are to mark their own encounters so they can use them as reminders for the next generation. So the next generation will say: "I won't forget the future place in God that I've never been to, because I know that I was not designed to stay here."

The world and the enemy try to get us to forget that there is a place in God designed for us. But God placed us here at this time because He knit revival in our DNA. We cannot forget that we were born for this time.

There's a story I heard once about a person whose adopted child stood in his crib one day, crying for his mommy. The adoptive mom came running in the room and said, "I'm here, baby." And the child said, "Not you. My real mommy." The woman was completely shocked. The child had no reference that the woman wasn't his real mother. Yet woven in the child's DNA was the unconscious knowing that even though he was growing up there, he was not being raised by his birth family.

The cry is, "If I forget you, O Jerusalem, let me not forget revival. I understand that I might have been born in a season in between. I understand that I might have been born at a time when I may not have experienced revival before, but there's something on the inside of me that longs for it."

We could be going about our day, our year. We could be going about our church existence, lifting our hands and bowing down. We could be going around saying all the right church stuff: "Hi, how are you doing?" "God bless you." "Thank You, Jesus." "I'm blessed and highly favored." We could be singing the songs, looking at the words on the screen, hearing some good preaching. Then one day God walks into the room and says: "Don't forget that you are not supposed to be living an existence in which you just think that going to church and coming home is the totality of what I want to do in your life. I have something greater. I understand that you might

have been born in a season when you haven't experienced a demonstration of My power. But there's something that I have woven into
your DNA. There's something that I planted on the inside of you
that will one day, out of the blue, cause you to lift your voice and say,
'Jesus! I know there's more than this. And I don't want to forget why
You sent me here on this earth at this time.'"

HE'S INTENTIONAL

God puts a people in a certain time to accomplish a certain thing.
It's His intention for those particular people to see what those who
came before them may not have gotten a chance to see. Entire generations participate in moving the plan of God forward. God doesn't
just think in days or years; He also thinks in generations. He's that
amazing. That God put us where He put us, which is two thousand
years after the death and burial of Jesus, means that we are not at
the beginning of a process. We are two thousand years closer to the
return of Christ than they were in the book of Acts, which means
God intentionally placed us in this time.

He could've placed us under the old covenant. He could have
placed us in the time when they observed the Law of Moses and
had to make all the bloody sacrifices, but He placed us in a day of
grace. And because of the time He has placed us in, our urgency
should increase.

> *God doesn't just think in days and years; He also thinks in
> generations.*

We are living in a time two thousand years after the first- and
second-century church, and they lived with great expectancy. That
should make us ask ourselves why we are not feeling that something
is drawing closer than ever before. The level of urgency for the early
church got so serious that Paul had to write and say, "Listen, don't
quit your jobs." (See 2 Thessalonians 3:6–15.) People were literally
being idle. They dropped everything, believing the coming of Christ
was upon them. They were thinking, "I don't need to work because

Jesus is coming at any point, and because He's coming, I don't even need a job. I don't need to pay my bills." Paul told them to continue to work. They lived with such an urgency. It's amazing that the further we get away from that time, the less urgent we've become.

But that's the opposite of the reaction we should have because we are thousands of years closer than they were. Our urgency should be increasing, not decreasing. If our urgency is not increasing, that means that we are out of alignment with God's will, Word, and plan. As a matter of fact, Peter had this to say:

> Most importantly, I want to remind you that in the last days scoffers will come, mocking the truth and following their own desires. They will say, "What happened to the promise that Jesus is coming again? From before the times of our ancestors, everything has remained the same since the world was first created."
>
> They deliberately forget that God made the heavens long ago by the word of his command, and he brought the earth out from the water and surrounded it with water. Then he used the water to destroy the ancient world with a mighty flood. And by the same word, the present heavens and earth have been stored up for fire. They are being kept for the day of judgment, when ungodly people will be destroyed.
>
> But you must not forget this one thing, dear friends: A day is like a thousand years to the Lord, and a thousand years is like a day. The Lord isn't really being slow about his promise, as some people think. No, he is being patient for your sake. He does not want anyone to be destroyed, but wants everyone to repent.
>
> —2 PETER 3:3–9

The reason Jesus has not yet come is because our God is so merciful that He is being patient. He is looking at the state of the world and knows that if He comes now, a whole lot of people are going to be in judgment. He does not want any to perish, so He is giving them more time. Jesus has not yet returned because of the mercy of God. He's not being slow concerning His promise.

Still, we should live with urgency because the Scripture goes on to say that we should be prepared because the day of the Lord is coming like a thief in the night (2 Pet. 3:10). No one will expect it. But we wait with great expectation.

We were placed in this time because God knew we would wait. He knew we would be the ones to remember His promise to bring revival. We remember that He said, "But then I will come and do for you all the good things I have promised, and I will bring you home again" (Jer. 29:10).

ABBA!

For all who are led by the Spirit of God are children of God. So you have not received a spirit that makes you fearful slaves. Instead, you received God's Spirit when he adopted you as his own children. Now we call him, "Abba, Father."

—Romans 8:14–15

And because we are his children, God has sent the Spirit of his Son into our hearts, prompting us to call out, "Abba, Father."

—Galatians 4:6

Just like the baby who cried out for his mother when he did not know he had another mother, it is the same with God, who prompts us to cry out, "Abba, Father," and who prompts us to cry out for revival. In Psalm 137 that next generation of Israelites said, "By the rivers of Babylon we sat and wept when we remembered Zion" (niv). A generation who had never seen Jerusalem was being prompted by the Spirit of God to cry out for revival. This is the challenge of intercession for us.

While we are here in this world, there's something about normalcy that gets to us after a while. A group of people is being boxed in by normal church, normal living, and normal things. We're being told we're doing too much, we're too loud, we're preaching too long, we're shouting too long, we're singing too long, our service is too long, we're praying too much. And we're questioned about the hope we have: "You still have faith for that? It hasn't happened." "Why are you still doing that?" "Why are you still giving? Just be normal. Just be like everybody else." When these things happen, there's something on the inside of us that says, "You are not my Father." There's something on the inside of us that says, "Give me my real Dad. I want my Father."

Why are you frustrated? Because the Spirit of God is prompting you to cry out for revival. Why can't you get comfortable at night? Because the Spirit of God is prompting you to cry out for revival. Why are you sensing that there's something more? Because the Spirit of God is prompting you to cry out. That's why we weep when we remember Zion.

RESPOND

You need to know you're not uncomfortable just to be uncomfortable. God has intentionally made you that way. It's His doing. He wants you to be dissatisfied with where you are. He wants you to want more. If you're wondering where the pin in your seat came from that causes you to jump up when you want to sit down and get comfortable, it came from God.

God is the One who has orchestrated the events in the world to drive the church to its knees. It is because of His prompting that His children are crying out for more.

We may not be the generation that was born living in the presence of God, but we hold on to the promise that He will come and bring revival. We have been put here for a reason. We were born for this moment. We may not have seen the manifestation of His presence, but we want it. And we won't stop until we see it.

How about you?

NOTES

CHAPTER 3—HE HEARS YOUR CRY

1. Merriam-Webster.com, s.v. "groan," accessed January 22, 2018, https://www.merriam-webster.com/thesaurus/groaning.

CHAPTER 4—FOLLOW THE PATHWAY

1. "About John G. Lake," John G. Lake Ministries, accessed January 22, 2018, http://www.jglm.org/john-g-lake/; see also Roberts Liardon, "John G. Lake," God's Generals, accessed January 22, 2018, http://godsgenerals.com/jlake/.

2. Chad Brand, ed., et al, *Holman Illustrated Bible Dictionary* (Nashville, TN: B&H Publishing Group, 2015), as quoted in Edward D. Andrews, *Evidence That You Are Truly Christian* (Cambridge, OH: Christian Publishing House, 2015), 272.

CHAPTER 6—NO SUBMISSION, NO POWER

1. Blue Letter Bible, s.v. *"arrabon,"* accessed January 24, 2018, https://www.blueletterbible.org/lang/lexicon/lexicon.cfm?Strongs=G728&t=KJV.

2. "Bible Verses About Holy Spirit as Engagement Ring," BibleTools.org, accessed January 24, 2018, https://www.bibletools.org/index.cfm/fuseaction/Topical.show/RTD/cgg/ID/5951/Holy-Spirit-as-Engagement-Ring.htm.

CHAPTER 8—STAY AND WAIT

1. Robert Jamieson, A. R. Fausset, and David Brown, *Commentary Critical and Explanatory on the Whole Bible*, "Acts 1," accessed January 24, 2018, http://www.biblestudytools.com/commentaries/jamieson-fausset-brown/acts/acts-1.html.

2. Blue Letter Bible, s.v. *"homothymadon,"* accessed January 24, 2018, https://www.blueletterbible.org/lang/Lexicon/Lexicon.cfm?strongs=G3661&t=KJV.

3. "Children's Question Room," Toyota, accessed January 24, 2018, http://www.toyota.co.jp/en/kids/faq/b/01/06/.

4. Rolls-Royce Raleigh, "How Long Does It Take to Build a Rolls-Royce?" Rolls-Royce Motor Cars Raleigh, December 12, 2014, http://blog.rolls-roycemotorcarsraleigh.com/long-take-build-rolls-royce/.

5. The account of Edward Miller is documented in Lila Terhune, *Cross Pollination* (Shippensburg, PA: Destiny Image, 1998), 4–10; see

also R. Edward Miller, *The Secrets of the Argentine Revival*, viewed at
Measure of Gold Revival Ministries, accessed January 24, 2018, http://
www.evanwiggs.com/revival/history/The%20Beginning%20of%20
the%20Great%20Argentine%20Revival.htm.

CHAPTER 9—CONTEND FOR THE FLAMES OF REVIVAL

1. Abigail Hess, "Here's Why Lottery Winners Go Broke," CNBC,
August 25, 2017, https://www.cnbc.com/2017/08/25/heres-why-lottery
-winners-go-broke.html.

2. *30 for 30: Broke*, ESPN.com, accessed January 24, 2018, http://
www.espn.com/30for30/film?page=broke.

3. David Margolick, "Elizabeth Eckford and Hazel Bryan: The Story
Behind the Photograph That Shamed America," *The Telegraph*, October
9, 2011, http://www.telegraph.co.uk/news/worldnews/northamerica
/8813134/Elizabeth-Eckford-and-Hazel-Bryan-the-story-behind-the
-photograph-that-shamed-America.html.

4. Michele Norris, "The Woolworth Sit-In That Launched a Movement," NPR.org, February 1, 2008, http://www.npr.org/templates/story
/story.php?storyId=18615556.

CHAPTER 10—A WORTHY HOST

1. *Ellicott's Commentary for English Readers*, "1 Samuel 6:19," accessed
January 24, 2018, http://biblehub.com/commentaries/1_samuel
/6-19.htm.

2. Robert Jamieson, A. R. Fausset, and David Brown, *Commentary
Critical and Explanatory on the Whole Bible*, s.v. "2 Samuel 6," accessed January 24, 2018, http://www.biblestudytools.com/commentaries/jamieson
-fausset-brown/2-samuel/2-samuel-6.html.

CHAPTER 13—IT HAPPENED BECAUSE IT'S HAPPENING

1. Orlando Sentinel Editorial Board, "Orlando Grieves With Las
Vegas," *Orlando Sentinel*, October 2, 2017, http://www.orlando
sentinel.com/opinion/os-ed-las-vegas-massacre-pulse-shooting
-20171002-story.html.

2. "The Most Visited Cities in the US," WorldAtlas.com, January 24,
2018, http://www.worldatlas.com/articles/the-most-visited-cities-in-the
-us.html.

3. Sandra Pedicini, "Visit Orlando: Record 68 Million People Visited
Last Year," *Orlando Sentinel*, May 11, 2017, http://www.orlandosentinel
.com/business/tourism/os-visit-orlando

-tourist-numbers-20170511-story.html; Jeff Kunerth, "Getting Bigger: Metro Orlando Grows to 2.3 Million," *Orlando Sentinel*, March 26, 2015, http://www.orlandosentinel.com/news/breaking-news/os-census -population-central-florida-20150326-story.html.

In a time when a lot of the information being promoted is contrary to the Word of God, this generation needs something more than just traditional church services. This generation needs to see a demonstration of God's power, and this has been found at Deeper Fellowship Church in Orlando, Florida, under the guidance of Pastor William McDowell. Miracles, signs, and wonders are happening literally week in and week out. These events are providing hope and truth to eliminate any doubt that the God we've heard about is real. The Bible says these signs shall follow those who believe (Mark 16:17), so our faith is rising to the occasion because of what's being demonstrated at Deeper Fellowship Church. I'm really excited about the release of this book, which shares miracles you wouldn't believe unless you read about them or saw them with your own eyes.

—TRAVIS GREENE
MULTIPLE GRAMMY AWARD–NOMINATED WORSHIP LEADER
LEAD PASTOR, FORWARD CITY CHURCH

God is using William McDowell and Deeper Fellowship Church to be a prophetic signpost in this generation. In the tension between seeking God's presence and seeking to be cool, they're favoring His presence. And God is honoring that with miracles. May you be infected with the spirit of faith that permeates this book.

—BOB SORGE
AUTHOR, *SECRETS OF THE SECRET PLACE*

From the moment I met William McDowell, humility and faithfulness oozed out of him. The same can be said when you begin to experience this book. It's truly an encouragement toward greater faith and a challenge to not miss what God has happening in your life!

—JOSH McCOWN
QUARTERBACK, NEW YORK JETS

I've been able to see the handicapped walk, the sick healed, and frowns turned to smiles. The atmosphere at Deeper Fellowship is hard to describe, but when you are present, you understand just how impactful and loving a home it is. What I love is how William doesn't move until he knows the Holy Spirit has moved in the way

He's supposed to. This book will give you a glimpse into what God is doing in our church and challenge you to go deeper.

—Tobias Harris
Forward, Los Angeles Clippers

The Bible eloquently speaks of God sending pastors who are after His own heart. Pastor William McDowell and the life-changing work happening at Deeper Fellowship perfectly epitomize what that looks like. He is a leader in full pursuit of the God who has called him. Anytime he stands to offer a testimony about the miracles Deeper is experiencing, it pushes me to continue ministering the pure and unadulterated Word of God—because that is ultimately what creates a space for heaven to kiss the earth. I'm sure that many across the globe can relate to this same push and inspiration; it's contagious.

It's Happening will further solidify to the world a fact that many have long known: Pastor William McDowell is indeed a host of God's presence and a general for the agenda of revival.

—Tasha Cobbs Leonard
Grammy Award–Winning Worship Leader

I am so excited about the miracles taking place at Deeper Fellowship Church and through Pastor William McDowell's ministry. He's shaking the culture and experiencing God's power on earth as it is in heaven and seeing wonderful miracles as a result. I love his heart for God. A church that stays in God's presence will always experience heaven! This book will turn hearts to God! I'm glad to call this man of God my friend!

—Erica Campbell
Host, Nationally Syndicated Radio Show *Get Up! Mornings With Erica Campbell*; Grammy Award–Winning Artist; Member, Chart-Topping Duo Mary Mary

It's hard to believe that I've known William McDowell for only a handful of years because the impact of his ministry on my life has been exponential. Much of my approach to music has been totally shifted by my conversations with William and by the hours of worship in the Father's presence facilitated through William's music.

From the many impactful conversations we've had, one statement stands out to me more than any other. He told me, "If we say what the Father says, He'll make a way for His word." That one sentence has reverberated in my life through the years, and I credit it with much of the success I've had as a Christian artist. It has taught me to dig deep into God when I write songs.

I'm grateful for William's ministry and his posture of obedience to the Father. I'm grateful for not only his friendship but also his ability to demonstrate a life poured out, a life tangibly connected to the heart of God. I know this book will greatly impact all who read it with open hearts, and I'm excited about the new season so many people will walk into because of it.

—DANNY GOKEY
GRAMMY AWARD–NOMINATED, AWARD–WINNING
CHRISTIAN ARTIST

In William McDowell's new book, *It's Happening*, he speaks on behalf of those seeking revival. Not only does he represent the revivalist accurately, but he also encourages those who don't share this appetite for a heavenly resurgence to change their diets. This book is a glorious recipe to encounter the miraculous and supernatural, which is exactly what our starving world needs at this moment in history. Knowing William personally, I'm not surprised at all by the rich content that saturates this book because it's really only a window into what he embodies and abides in daily. Like every other aspect of his ministry, this book is a necessity in our pursuit of Jesus.

—CHRIS DURSO
AUTHOR, *THE HEIST: HOW GRACE ROBS US OF OUR SHAME*

Pastor William McDowell has given his life to listening to the Holy Spirit's voice, as he has fashioned prophetic songs that give the family of God words to express their deepest feelings of worship. That same ability to hear the Holy Spirit and write songs of worship has found expression in revelatory teaching and preaching that has produced a faith to believe for the supernatural as a regular visitation of the Holy Spirit in their home church.

—BISHOP JOSEPH L. GARLINGTON SR.
FOUNDING PASTOR, COVENANT CHURCH OF PITTSBURGH
PRESIDING BISHOP, RECONCILIATION! MINISTRIES INTERNATIONAL

Pastor William McDowell is a trailblazing leader in the world of worship and a true friend of mine. He is already known for his historic record within the music industry, but in this book we are able to see another passion of William's. *It's Happening* reveals William's heart for the things of God. This book ignites passion within the reader and helps to give inspiration and education on miracles, signs, and wonders. This is a must-read for every believer who wants to go deeper in his or her walk with God!

—Matthew L. Stevenson III
Senior Pastor, All Nations Worship Assembly

It's happening! What a great reminder that revival isn't just something of the past or the future, but it's happening right now. This book is water for the spiritually dry and an anthem for those who desperately long for a move of God. I'm convinced that wherever these pages are being turned, fires of fervor are going to be set ablaze. I'm thankful that William would write these words. I'm even more grateful that he is living them out.

—Levi Lusko
Pastor, Fresh Life Church, a Multisite Church in Montana
and Utah; Author, *Swipe Right: The Life-and-Death Power
of Sex and Romance* and *Through the Eyes of a Lion*

The earth is experiencing the crest of a wave of awakening. Like a spear piercing through the darkness, a tribe of kingdom worshippers is marching the breadth and width of the earth, exercising kingdom authority and experiencing the signs and wonders of the kingdom. At the tip of that spear God has positioned Pastor William McDowell with a mantle of miracles and a grace to release revival among the nations. The grace God has put on his life is a unique, threefold cord of prophetic worship, fervent prayer, and holy manifestation of God's presence. The message he carries calls a generation of sons and daughters closer to the heart of God. As a man after God's own heart, Pastor William is marked by the humility and kindness that he exudes while carrying this mantle of revival across the nations.

—Bishop Kevin Wallace
Senior Pastor, Redemption to the Nations Church

"This is very uncommon and extraordinary and should be treasured." Those were the words that fell from my lips the first time I experienced Deeper Fellowship and the Habitation Conference they host each year. Pastor William and his team are experiencing the realities of heaven being manifest in the earth.

If you've ever been around him, you know that Pastor William McDowell is not a musical artist; he is a worshipper and pursuer of God who is a carrier of contagious faith. Within the first few pages of *It's Happening* you will be challenged to new levels of faith by the testimonies, will be encouraged to release the presumptions you have about how church is supposed to be, and will discover the simple, yet profound, pathway of experiencing God up close and personally. What you will discover more than anything is that Pastor William and churches such as Deeper are becoming the new norm! This book is a *must*-read! And as you read it, get ready—"it" will begin to happen in you!

—BISHOP TONY MILLER
PASTOR, THE GATE CHURCH

Every now and then someone special emerges, and something special happens in their world. William McDowell has developed a literal "open heaven" with praise, worship, prayer, and the Word. It's happening—the book of Acts experience of miracles, signs, and wonders. It's happening—the outpouring of God's Spirit the prophet Joel proclaimed. It's happening—what Isaiah prophesied, that the glory of God would manifest. It's happening! The power of God is being released with tangible evidence.

—BISHOP TUDOR BISMARK
FOUNDER, JABULA—NEW LIFE MINISTRIES INTERNATIONAL
PASTOR, NEW LIFE COVENANT CHURCH

I have been blessed by the mantle of praise and worship William McDowell is known for, and I have been to Deeper Fellowship Church and experienced firsthand the power of God in the atmosphere under his leadership. What's happening there is a beautiful fulfillment of God's promises in Acts 2:17 and Mark 16:17–19. I pray the accounts documented in this book will bring life to the reader and ignite faith like wildfire within the church worldwide. To God be the glory!

—JACKIE PATILLO
PRESIDENT, EXECUTIVE DIRECTOR, GOSPEL MUSIC ASSOCIATION

Every generation prays for revival but forgets that every revival needs a revivalist. I believe William McDowell has been called to be a modern David in this post-Christian culture to usher the honor and weight of God to this current generation. *It's Happening* highlights the wonders of God's Word and the power of a *yes*!

—DAVID S. JACQUES
PASTOR, THE KINGDOM CHURCH

I have been listening to the worship music of William McDowell for many years, and for me it's not just about listening or singing along; it's always brought life-changing moments of worship in God's presence. You cannot turn on William's music and not be affected by the tangible presence of heaven coming through the airwaves. I believe his ability to transform a room with worship is attributed not just to his unique and absolutely fantastic songwriting skills but also to a life dedicated to pursuing the heart of the Father.

When you listen to his songs, you can tell he has had an encounter with God, which is reflected in the deep passion for God that comes out of his mouth when he sings. This deep-felt passion is also communicated when he preaches. You can always hear the heart of God toward His people through the word he declares and ministers.

It's not surprising that his ministry has become global, effortlessly crossing ethnic and cultural barriers. In my experience I have found that when you have a ministry like this, it's not uncommon to see miracles taking place because worship has the ability to bring God into an environment, and when God's presence shows up, miracles happen. I am sure that reading this book will transform your life, your ministry, and your community because this isn't just a man thing; it's a God thing, and it's happening!

—BISHOP JOHN FRANCIS
SENIOR PASTOR, RUACH CITY CHURCH

I've had the unique opportunity to be a firsthand witness to William's life and the events and stories this book documents. I've heard the prayers he has prayed. I've seen the tears he has cried, the seeds he has sown, and the sacrifices he has made, all so a generation will live in the place of God encounters. I believe the story of *It's Happening* is possible only because God found a man on the earth who was willing to surrender everything and not settle for anything less than a move of God. William has never pursued God's hand, but he has always pursued God's heart. Subsequently God has responded by demonstrating His power. I'm privileged to call William my best friend, and his life is proof that God honors private devotion with public demonstration. *It's Happening* will give you a glimpse into what I believe God wants to do in every city and in every nation. I pray the Holy Spirit stirs within your heart a desire for the bombardment of heaven in your midst.

—CALEB GRANT
ASSOCIATE PASTOR, DEEPER FELLOWSHIP CHURCH

If you relegate William McDowell to just the writer of hit worship songs, you've missed the mark. He is a servant of God who hears the frequency of heaven and repeats what he has heard in the earth. Because of that sensitivity William has been tasked with housing/leading a move of God in Orlando that has changed the landscape of normal church forever. The same grace that rests on William has been transmitted to everyone who comes in contact with that anointing. *It's Happening* is a glimpse into the realities of miracles, signs, and wonders that are taking place at Deeper Fellowship Church and the posture they have assumed to welcome and sustain God's presence. Read this book and allow your life to be altered for the better. Read it and find the altar that will allow that same power to hit your home, church, business, and life.

—BISHOP JASON NELSON
AWARD-WINNING GOSPEL ARTIST
PASTOR, GREATER BETHLEHEM TEMPLE

I've been privileged to have a front-row seat to many different moves of God over the last fifty years of my life. Revivals in various parts of the world have produced incredible miracles through men and women who walked closely with God. I've seen great outpourings where I've witnessed various signs that would make me wonder. In other places I've seen the creative release of worship that would take those of us present to exhilarating realms of God's glory that left us speechless. I've longed to see it again! I live with an expectation of "more of God" because I know that more is available than what most of our churches are experiencing.

I've known William McDowell for several years, and I know his gift and passion for God's presence are at a level that most people don't have the courage to pursue. William is simply a lover of Jesus, and he has made God's presence a priority in his life. As a result, he's stumbled into the reward of the man who would diligently seek God. Every time I'm with him in a service, I remember revivals I've experienced before, and a phrase rises up inside of me: "It's happening!"

I began to get phone calls and texts from William giving me testimonies of miracles breaking out from week to week in his church. I texted back to him on one occasion, "It's happening!" I had no idea that the church had started making that declaration as the river began to rise in their church. It's happening! It's happening!

There is a fresh wave of God's presence with the release of miracles and wonders swiftly coming to the earth. Are you ready? If you want to know what it looks like, read this book and jump into the river!

—DAVID BINION
AWARD-WINNING WORSHIP LEADER, SONGWRITER

God has entrusted to Pastor William McDowell and Deeper Fellowship Church (DFC) a beautiful and genuine move of the Holy Spirit. A fresh anointing is being poured out of an open heaven. I, myself, have experienced this unique and growing spiritual stir at DFC. Standing there worshipping in a room filled with surrendered hearts, I could feel the weight of glory pressing upon us. The sweet presence of Jesus becomes so real in that atmosphere. And there is evidence. Souls are saved, bodies are healed, and lives are forever transformed. I know that as you read *It's Happening*, your faith will be stirred, and your hunger for more of God will grow. Heaven will mark you, and you will learn to steward the presence of the Holy Spirit. You will become a habitation of power. May what is happening there happen in you.

—DAVID DIGA HERNANDEZ
EVANGELIST; AUTHOR, 25 *TRUTHS ABOUT DEMONS AND SPIRITUAL WARFARE AND CARRIERS OF THE GLORY*

It's Happening is a fresh, bold approach to the reality and manifestation of revival. The move of God, the outpouring of the Spirit, and the gifts of the Spirit are not relegated to the pages of the Bible or to past historical accounts. They're happening now! My friend Pastor William McDowell is at the forefront of a generation that is uncovering an authentic and relevant move of God. This book will not only stir your hunger for revival but cause you to become the revival.

—Jonathan Miller
Lead Pastor, New Beginnings Church

In a world where many are seeking attention, fame, and fortune merely for themselves, it never ceases to amaze me when I encounter people who are more concerned about God's glory than their own and who still value and desire the presence of God. William McDowell is one of those godly people. In his music and his ministry there are a simplicity and sincerity that attract God. It's clear that he hungers and thirsts for more of Him. You know a tree by the fruit it bears, and there is much good fruit in the life and ministry of William McDowell. God's presence is truly in the midst of Deeper Fellowship. Continue, my friend. Continue to hunger and thirst for more.

—Andre Ward
Olympic Champion; Former World Boxing Champion;
HBO Boxing Analyst

Whenever God wants to influence a people, He'll find a person. If He wants to impact a community, He will search for a praying people. And when He wants to transform the nations, He'll find a few apostolic churches. It gives me great joy to know God has found a man, a group of people, and an apostolic church in Orlando, Florida— Deeper Fellowship Church (DFC), led by Pastor William McDowell.

I came in contact with these precious people of God in a very unique way. The first thing I saw by revelation during worship there was a "river" rising and eventually flowing out from DFC into the city, impacting and transforming four major spheres of influence in it. I have watched with amazement the unscripted and unorganized move of God that's happening there with special miracles. It is happening! You can now experience it for yourself!

—Sam Oye
Pastor, The Transforming Church

With the humility of a lamb and the glory-filled power of a lion, Pastor William is truly a general of this generation. Not only have I been a firsthand witness to countless miracles under his ministry, but I likewise witnessed his personal integrity, passion for God's heart, and love for God's people. Out of the clamoring collection of voices in the world that are vying for your attention, Pastor William's voice is one that is proven and worthy to be attended to.

—Tony Jones
Pastor, Fellowship Church

I have personally and very intimately witnessed someone who has lived his life for a singular purpose for most of my life. I don't remember and can't recall a time over our twenty-plus years of brotherhood when William McDowell did not desire God to move. I'm not talking about a casual encounter but a radical one, the kind that people talk about for generations to come! William has been on the edge, awaiting and pointing to what has finally arrived. What is happening now happened to him some time ago, and now God has raised him up to help us enter into it! God has moved upon someone yet again, and that move has begun a movement. It indeed is happening. Let's not miss it, but let's seize what we are seeing! Let's go all in!

—Jason McMullen
Executive Pastor, Deeper Fellowship Church

As you hold *It's Happening* in your hand, understand that you are now connected to the anointing that is upon William McDowell. He is a proven and seasoned vessel of God who carries a deep prophetic insight with an apostolic clarity, and he is trusted by God to dispense the supernatural power and presence of God in the earth, as it was in the days of the book of Acts. This is not a normal book full of well-thought-out information. This book is literally a point of contact with heaven that will release an impartation in your world that will cause what is happening at Deeper Fellowship Church to happen to you. By the time you are done taking all of this in, you will undoubtedly say, "It's happening in my world too."

—Patrick Kiteley
Pastor, Rain Church

Pastor William McDowell is an amazing friend and a most-esteemed kingdom partner. His love for God's people is unparalleled and shows in everything he does. Our society has faced some challenging times, and we have seen the hand of God shift things in the earth. Even with the shift, Pastor McDowell has maintained a keen level of precision in leading God's people because his ear remains fastened to the mouth of God. Pastor McDowell is a refreshing and much-needed vessel who understands the methodology required to release the power of God in the earth realm. I am a firm believer that the earth will yield the increase of Pastor McDowell's anointing for years to come.

—JOHN F. HANNAH
SENIOR PASTOR, NEW LIFE COVENANT CHURCH SOUTHEAST

In the years that I worked with William McDowell, I was blessed to experience the presence of God in such a unique way. William has an unparalleled gift of ushering people into God's presence, then virtually disappearing so that God can work in the hearts of the people gathered there without distraction or pretense. I have witnessed firsthand God's supernatural power working through William's music ministry and through Deeper Fellowship. I'm so glad that even a sample of God's miraculous works is finally being shared in this book. Let it ignite in each of us the faith that revival has come and that God is here to work in and through us!

—EJ GAINES
VICE PRESIDENT OF MARKETING, MOTOWN GOSPEL

My experience with the ministry of William McDowell has been powerful and enriching. His passion for God and his worship have impacted me and the church I lead in unbelievable ways!

—JOHN JENKINS
PASTOR, FIRST BAPTIST CHURCH OF GLENARDEN

Deeper Fellowship Church was birthed out of the most unique premise: William McDowell wanted to create a space where time, personality, and pageantry didn't matter, only the presence of God. What has transpired from day one has been something I personally have never seen before: a church where worship is unforced, the people are passionate, and absolutely anything can happen at any moment.

Every person God has ever used to make a difference in the earth has had to be comfortable with being different. And William McDowell is no exception. He believed that if God could find a people who were willing to linger in His presence and believe for the impossible, anything would happen. And he was right! It's happening!

—Hart Ramsey
Senior Pastor, Northview Christian Center

Known for bringing the power and presence of God into our cars, living rooms, and churches through his gift of music, William McDowell will now help deliver it through the printed page. I pray that as you read this book, the stories will help you believe for revival in your home, church, and community. With this book we get to see the Spirit behind the sound.

—Micahn Carter
Lead Pastor, Together Church

For years I've studied revival. After every book, article, or documentary I read or watched, I would often say, "Jesus, let it happen here in Central Florida." I believe a holy invitation has come from heaven, and it's happening now!

Many of you know William as an award-winning worship leader, but before any of that happened, he was hidden and gave God His *yes* in the secret place. Over and over I have watched him say yes. He's a man of zero compromise, deep wisdom, purity, humility, and integrity when no one is watching. I believe because of that obedience he has touched the heart of God deeply and therefore continues to impact everyone around him. God used him to change the course of my family's life, and we've felt the consuming fire of Jesus evident at Deeper Fellowship. It truly is happening!

—Theo Koulianos Jr.
Pastor, The Answer Church

There are some people you meet who immediately show you that God has more to offer. Pastor William McDowell is one of those people. He is a model for revival. I believe the rarity of his integrity, humility, and commitment to the plan of God is directly tied to the manifestations seen in his ministry. The culture of his life has opened the door for the heavens to pour out the impossible. It is my belief that God doesn't want to do the impossible just in him. Pastor William's breakthroughs are meant to cause faith to rise in you to chase the move of God for your life as well. My prayer is that as you read this book and pursue the presence of God, you will be provoked to look at your life and give God your *yes* so you also will be able to say, "It's happening!"

—Josh Hart
Pastor, Liberty Church

As a fellow pastor in the Orlando area, I have seen firsthand how God is using Pastor William McDowell in our city and abroad. Through the powerful ministry of Pastor William McDowell a fresh wind of revival has come to our city. Pastor William has made himself available to be used by the Holy Spirit and without restriction has created an atmosphere for the miraculous to take place. Pastor William McDowell's heart for worship and pure desire to see God move in people's lives have been instrumental in creating such an environment. I have experienced the sweet presence of the Holy Spirit at Deeper Fellowship Church, and in this book he shares how we can experience this in our own lives. When we focus on pursuing the very presence of God, heaven touches earth, and lives are changed, healed, set free, and restored. It's happening!

—Riva Tims
Senior Pastor, Majestic Life Church

Pastor William McDowell has always had a passion for God and engaged in an unrelenting pursuit of the things of God! I have known William for over thirty years, and even when he was a young teenager, it was evident that he had been given a musical gift and had a calling on his life to touch the world. It is no surprise that he has been raised up as one of the leading worship leaders in this generation.

Now as a senior pastor, William has chosen to courageously lead his congregation outside the lines of tradition and conformity, and by so doing, they are experiencing what it truly looks like when heaven touches earth! I am honored to know William and to see how God is using him to bring His kingdom to earth. May "it" happen *everywhere*!

—John W. Stevenson
Apostle and Senior Pastor, HEIRS Covenant Church

Pastor McDowell is a servant leader, and this book is a must-read testament to his and his congregation's faith combining with works to bring forth revival. *It's Happening* is a testimony we all should read.

—PHIL THORNTON
SENIOR VICE PRESIDENT AND GENERAL MANAGER, RCA
INSPIRATION

I had not heard of William McDowell in 2009. I was in Walmart walking down the gospel music aisle when I heard the Lord say, "Stop!" So I stopped immediately, not knowing what I was looking for. After feeling prompted to look to my left, I did so, and there it was, the album *As We Worship Live* by William McDowell. The purchase of this album began a three-month period of weekly supernatural visitations from angels and even the Lord Himself, and through that process God birthed me into full-time ministry.

When I discovered years later that William had started pastoring a church, I was so excited that I moved my entire family to a different city just to be close enough to attend the church when my ministry was not on the road. There aren't many people outside the ones written about in the book of Acts who have had that much of an impact on my life. To paraphrase the apostle Peter in 2 Peter 1:16, I am an eyewitness of the revival that is taking place in the church that William leads. I can say with certainty, "It's happening!"

—JONATHAN FERGUSON
FERGUSON GLOBAL MINISTRIES

I have had the unique opportunity of walking with William as a partner in his recorded music ministry. We have spent much time over the last ten years working to impart to the masses the music God gave him. I have always said that you learn the truth about artists during the process of promoting an album. When other artists would have chosen to self-promote, William consistently chooses to exalt Jesus. He is one of the most authentic people I know, someone who is sure of what he has been put on earth to do. The posture of his heart is to follow God's will and purpose for his life, which keeps him in a relentless pursuit of the presence of God. That is where he is leading anyone who chooses to follow him—into God's presence.

Through the revival happening at Deeper Fellowship, God is using William to remind us that He is still with us, He still hears us, He still can, and He still will. Many people believe things not because of what they have been told but because of what they have seen. This revival has given the unbeliever proof that God still gives sight to the blind, a voice to the voiceless, and legs to those who couldn't walk. Many people have walked into Deeper Fellowship with a burden and have walked out with proof that God is real and wants to move in their lives.

May the proof taking place at Deeper activate your faith to believe that if revival can happen there, it can happen anywhere. Modern-day miracles do exist! Persuasion is not necessary when there is a demonstration of the power of God. "It's happening!"

—GINA MILLER
VICE PRESIDENT AND GENERAL MANAGER, ENTERTAINMENT ONE

There's an obvious anointing on William that comes from a deep well of time spent with God. He walks through this life at a slower pace, trading performance for a divine move of God. He's not interested in accolades, only anointing. He's a true friend who has cried with me, prayed with me, and encouraged me. I love how he constantly pushes those around him to press in close and listen to the voice of God. I know God has written these words on William's heart.

—JEREMY FOSTER
PASTOR, HOPE CITY